HERE ON THE ISLAND

HERE ON
THE ISLAND

Being an Account of
a Way of Life Several Miles Off the Maine Coast

Text and photographs by
Charles Pratt

Drawings by Harold S. van Doren

HARPER & ROW, PUBLISHERS
New York, Evanston, San Francisco, London

ACKNOWLEDGMENTS

In writing the chapter on fishing, I have been helped very much by the following sources:
"Territories of the Lobsterman" by James M. Acheson, *Natural History,* April 1972.
About Lobsters by T. M. Prudden, The Bond Wheelwright Company, Freeport, Maine, 1962.
Article by Robin Alden in *Island Ad-Vantages,* Special Fishing Supplement, August 4, 1972.

C.P.

FIRST EDITION

Designed by Patricia Dunbar

For Julie and Mike

CONTENTS

One sunny, relaxed Sunday morning several years ago, I was sitting with a group of friends on the porch of a house at the beach, and my attention was drawn to one of the company who sat quietly under a white umbrella; the moment of repose was special to the quality of my friend, and, even more than most moments, it was transitory. I went into my sneaky photographer's dance —casually (oh, so casually) getting the camera from the corner of the porch, removing the lens cap, being careful to make no sudden moves which would attract attention but watching my quarry out of the corner of my eye, fearing that at any moment he would start and bound away. After a few pointings and clickings at other things to allow me to get a focus on something at an equivalent distance and to disguise the real reason for the camera, I panned slowly and casually to him, paused and made the exposure. It was a familiar ritual. I liked the contact print which resulted, and it wasn't until I made the first enlarged print that I noticed that there was a special smile on my friend's face, as he stared out into the middle distance of the dune grass, which wasn't completely justified by the tranquillity of our surroundings. Later, when I asked him about it, he said that yes, he had seen me sneaking up on him, had recognized that I liked the way he sat under the umbrella and had decided to make me a gift of his appearance at that moment.

I thank the Island for holding still.

HERE ON THE ISLAND

A patch of moss
Detail

Woods on the west side

The Small cemetery, near Rich's Cove

A meadow near Rich's Cove
A lichen-covered rock in winter grass

A corner of one of the cemeteries

Harold and Elthea Turner's house

The cliffs on the south shore

Boom Beach

The base of one of the south shore cliffs

The face of a rock at low tide

High tide
A tide pool in a seaweed-covered rock

A cove on the western shore

A cobble beach

The Thoroughfare and Phil's boat

One of the deer

The carcass of a deer on the south shore—probably shot and left by a poacher

Feeding herring gull

The nesting island

Bill Stevens and Pat Haynes on the nesting island

Eider duck eggs

membered as the places where, a generation or more ago, sheep were grazed or gull eggs collected. Some were then inhabited the year round, and one— York Island (just outside of Rich's Cove, where we lived that first year on the Island)—held a regular little community until about forty years ago.

The ledges, alternately covered and uncovered by the tides, lie off all the coasts in such a complicated jumble that it is dangerous for all except those who know the water very well to circumnavigate the Island at less of a distance than a mile from the shore. I really doubt that there is another island on the Maine coast which is so surrounded by treachery; thinking geologically, it was either an unusually broad mountain top with lots of complicated little valleys and pinnacles as you started down from the summit or else the land didn't sink quite enough for the water to cover it completely.

The islands of the Maine coast tend to be oblong and run roughly northeast to southwest, the axial direction of the valleys before they drowned and became sea bottom. As the tendency of the coast is east-west, this means that the northern ends of the islands point inland and are relatively sheltered and that the southern shores are exposed to the sea. Up the bay this doesn't make much difference, but on an outer island like ours the northern shore, which is sheltered from the full force of the Atlantic, has an entirely different look from the open southern shore. The northern and western shores recede gradually to the water line, and the tide, which rises and falls anywhere from eight to ten feet twice a day, is measured horizontally by its movement over gravel and pebble beaches and mud flats. The seaweed and the marine animals of this intertidal area live under a relatively gentle set of conditions. On the southern outer coast, the force of the sea over the ages has worn away the slopes of the drowned mountain to produce cliffs which get to be a hundred feet high and a different set of intertidal conditions. The highest of these cliffs are on the western half of the southern coast, and they're about as dramatic as any in New England. On Eastern Head is a place called Thunder Gulch, where the sea roars into a long narrow indentation in the cliff and, under some sea and tide conditions, bounces up about fifty feet into your face as you stand at the edge of the pine forest.

Boom Beach is the other natural wonder of the Island. Basically, the shore in this part of Maine is either solid rock, broken-up rock or mud; sand beaches are rare, because there hasn't been geological time enough for the sea to grind up the rock that fine. The rock which forms the beaches varies in size from pebbles through cobblestones, through flat pieces of shale to rocks which can be properly called small boulders. Boom Beach is made up of these last to a considerable depth; it lies on the southern part of the eastern shore and is as exposed to the full Atlantic as the cliffs on the southern coast. After a good storm most everybody gathers here to watch the sea smash in and roll the boulders about, making the earth shake. You can feel Boom Beach at these times all the way across the Island in town, over three miles away. There's an old expression, "the rote," which I'd heard once or twice but which hadn't really registered. It means the sound of the sea breaking on rock; and traveling on the sea at night or in the fog, it's useful as an indication of your exact location, if you know where you are generally. If you didn't know where you were at all, it could be the most frightening sound in the world. It's one thing to hear this noise from the sea and be scared or at least made wary, but if you're given to flights of fancy you could get pretty spooked-up over being on an eighteen-square-mile island which is shaken pretty regularly by the sea driving in on one part of it.

There are three populations. About two dozen people live on the Island the whole time, six of them children. An almost equal number leave the Island in November to return at the end of March, spending the midwinter months on the nearby mainland, either in their own or rented second homes. All of this group, I think, consider the Island to be their real home, and their connections to it are almost as deep as those of the year-round group. Starting in July, like birds of bright plumage, the summer people begin to arrive; it's practically impossible to tell how many there are, as they come and go, some being renters and some owners, but I heard it estimated that, for most of the summer, the population of the Island grows to about two hundred.

Only a fifth of the approximately one hundred habitable houses on the Island are inhabited in the winter, and only eleven of these for the full twelve months. Most of the remainder are inhabited by summer residents and year-round transients, but about fourteen remain uninhabited, although they are owned.

Most of the people have more than one occupation; in a very real sense, they all are primarily occupied with living on the Island, and this requires each to have a collection of skills and a willingness to divide up time worthy of a frontiersman. For instance, Jack MacDonald is a fisherman, but he spent most of one summer building his new house; you might say that Harold Turner is retired, but he runs the mailboat from November through March and spent most of a recent winter dynamiting post holes and helping to fill the holes with electric poles. Nobody is quite sure what he will be doing for the next twelve months except that by doing a number of things he will try to live on the Island and keep it and himself—as part of it—going. Between the two dozen totally year-round residents, all of the necessary or useful occupations are filled—fisherman, mechanic, schoolteacher, roadworker, post mistress, storekeeper, school-bus driver, mailboat operator.

There are a few couples who live off-island but stay often enough and long enough to qualify as kind of permanent transients: Bill Kirk, a retired clergyman, and his wife, Mary; Lawrence Cousins, who runs a garage on the mainland, his wife, children and grandchildren, who by turns occupy a camp down on the pond almost every weekend throughout the year; and Julie and me. We averaged about ten days on the Island out of every month during the year I was on, except for July and August, when we stayed all the time.

It's a pretty complicated, varied group. As I've said, the main occupation is the Island.

Roughly speaking, there are five clusters of houses on the Island. The town, on the northern half of the eastern coast, is pretty obviously located at the best anchorage nearest the Main, seven miles away. Its harbor is formed between Kimball's Island and the Island shore about a hundred yards from it and is really a passage and not a harbor. It's called the Thoroughfare and was impassable from the north entrance until 1958, when the obstructing sandbar was dredged, whereupon the town built itself a dock toward the southern end. There are thirty-five buildings in town, spread out for about three-quarters of a mile along the road which runs parallel to the water: a general store, a library (donated in memory of a summer resident), a post office, a church, a schoolhouse, a firehouse, a building to house the Island generator, a self-service gasoline pump and a couple of kerosene storage tanks.

Just north of the Thoroughfare is the Point, a group of about ten large nineteenth-century "cottages," most of them connected by boardwalks. The Point has its own dock, communal garage, post office and tennis courts. There are ten or more summer houses in the general area of the Point complex, scattered in among the pines and more or less connected in style and function to it. There is a road which, in its various states of surface, goes around the Island, and the Point community is isolated about a half mile down a dirt road from this main thoroughfare. It is, of course, deserted in the winter.

There are scattered houses on the east side for about two miles to the head of the pond. Three of these two dozen houses were occupied during the winter—one of them, on Rich's Cove, by us—and another one was occupied from

March to November. At the northern end of the pond there is a long meadow sloping up to an ample barn and an early-nineteenth-century farmhouse, now owned by a summer resident. It is one of the great prospects of the world but only slightly more beautiful than most other places on the Island.

The road runs between the pond and the eastern shore, past Boom Beach, which you reach by walking over a slight rise, and on to Head Harbor. This is the main harbor of the southern coast, facing straight out to sea, and there are a dozen houses here, five of them occupied during the summer and one of them intermittently during the fall and spring. After Head Harbor the road turns to dirt and shortly enters the park, which comprises about sixty percent of the Island, including most of the southern coast and the western side about halfway up its length. There is a small campground at Duck Harbor on the western coast. The northern park boundary meets the western coast just south of Moore's Harbor, which has five summer houses on its shores, all of them occupied during July and August. The road continues north to town and becomes paved just south of it. The circuit of the Island is about fourteen miles.

The salt-water barrier, rather than any peculiarities of environment, determines the animal life on the Island. Richard Manville did a study of the Island's vertebrates in 1964; he had previously done similar studies of two islands elsewhere in North America, and he uses two of these islands as comparative samples. One had been connected to the mainland by a mile-long causeway through salt water for nine years previous to his study and the other is isolated by a mile-wide stretch of fresh water which freezes over in the winter. On the basis of comparison of the number of mainland species found on these tenuously connected islands with the number of mainland species found on the Island, which is seven miles from the mainland, he concludes: "It seems evident that to many mammals, as well as freshwater fishes and herptiles [snakes and frogs], 6 miles or more of salt water have proved to be an insurmountable barrier." Deer seem to be the notable exception to this rule, having been sighted swimming in the Gulf of Maine quite far from shore.

Apart from deer (about which, more later), Manville reports the presence, among terrestrial mammals, of shrews, moles, bats, mice, meadow voles, muskrats, weasels, mink, otters and red squirrels. Snowshoe hares are in abundance, although I never saw any (which doesn't really prove anything). I did see a mink go across the road down at the foot of the pond once, and there were reports of the presence of a fisher, which is an extremely rare relative of the weasel, about four feet long and known for its ferocity.

In spring Maurice Barter and I puzzled over some tracks he saw in the sand of the road leading down to the creek where he had hauled his lobster boat up for the winter ("Lord," he said, "wonder what'll come on here next?") and we considered that it might be a bear for the two days we continued to see fresh tracks, but got hold of a track book and found out that it was probably an otter. Out in the waters of the Island the mammals include porpoises, harbor seals and pilot whales (or blackfish), which are about ten feet long. The largest of the whales—the right whale—is sighted occasionally as close as a few miles out to sea from the Island.

Manville reports that in the pond can be found landlocked salmon, brook trout, smelt, eels and nine-spined sticklebacks, which are "extremely abundant but small" (thank goodness!). Smelt fishing is a traditional noncommercial activity on this part of the Maine coast, mostly for the salt-water smelts which come up into the brooks to spawn in the spring. John Cousins and Bob Turner and I went after the smelts in the pond one April night, rowing from the Cousinses' camp up a quarter mile to the mouth of Bull Brook and hoping to get some with a dip net, as you can when they congregate there; it was a beautiful night, and we had a good time but didn't get any smelts.

There are green and garter snakes, salamanders, frogs and spring peepers. All in all, the list is smaller than on the nearest section of mainland, and many animals—like the porcupine and skunk—haven't found their way across. The water is no barrier to the birds, however, and Manville's list of them is long. Being in no way an ornithologist, I was particularly conscious of the land birds which I'd grown to associate with Maine because they had been part of Maine summers all my life—like the song sparrow I heard one day in the last week of April and knew winter was over—and the birds I'd never known in Maine, like the ravens which seemed to be around Rich's Cove in abundance. There is a bald eagle which nests on the southern end of the Great Meadow, a large swampy area on the way up Champlain Mountain, and at least one osprey, which returns every year to its nest atop the spindle marking a ledge at the southern end of the Thoroughfare. On sheltered flats sandpipers hunt at low tide, and I spent a little time trying to sneak up on the great blue heron which hung out around Nat's Cove and another heron which occasionally came over to Rich's Cove, without any results I'd care to show here. Pheasants were introduced on the Island in the 1890s but evidently failed to survive, as the last one was sighted in 1959; there are woodcock about, however.

The most evident bird is, of course, the seagull, and they are so numerous that they become indistinguishable from the general scene, until they start a flurry of feeding over bait fish moving inshore at high tide or bait thrown from a fishing boat. Near them at these times you can see how their static calm when standing on the shore, or their calm grace in the air, changes into a truly impressive savagery—only to change back into a graceful Maine cool after they have gotten what they want, or as they retire with dignity after they have failed in the object of a specific dive. Cormorants are around, but I don't remember seeing as many of them as I did when I spent summers further in toward the heads of the bays—probably because they tend to go inshore to feed during the day and then fly out in long lines to the outer small bare islands, like the ones surrounding the Island, in the evening. The Island is out to sea enough for there to be open-water birds nearby, and I have heard reports of large clouds of shearwaters skimming close over the waves nearby.

Of the ducks which winter in Maine, there are about seven species which hang around the Island in close to the town dock as well as out in the bay. The many fresh-water streams emptying into the surrounding salt water must provide a pleasant habitat, and all of the ducks come up into the mouths of these streams at high tide to drink. The breeding grounds of most of these —old squaws, goldeneyes, buffleheads, mergansers, black ducks, and so on —are in the Arctic, and the Maine coast is within their range of migration, but there is one species, the eider, of which the females at least stick around all year.

My principal guide to the wildlife on the Island was Bill Stevens, the park ranger, who stayed on that winter and worked on the roads. Bill was born in interior Maine and raised by a father who spent a good deal of time hunting and fishing. He went to the University of Maine and studied forestry, until he found out that forestry had more to do with the commercial harvesting of trees than anything else and switched to wildlife studies. He wanted to spend time in the woods, and, after getting his B.S. in the mid-sixties, it was natural that he would try to accomplish this end by becoming a park ranger. He came onto the Island to help in a deer-population study, became ranger, and in the ensuing four years has been drawn deep into the Island. He would like to be a game biologist, which he cannot very well become by living on the Island, entirely removed from an academic environment, but he also feels that he is growing more and more attached to the place each year. His conflict is further complicated by the fact that ranger duty is almost entirely police work now and has little to do with the wilderness, where Bill would like to be if he doesn't stay on the Island. For various complicated reasons the park is somewhat in disrepute on the Island, which complicated Bill's life when he first came on. By now he is a real part of the community (and, incidentally, remains so even though he stands up for the park on many issues).

Bill and his dog, Bitsy, and I spent the better part of one day in early April sneaking up on ducks. It was clear that he and Bitsy had done things like this a lot together. Drawing near the shore on the path through the woods, Bill issued no commands, however quiet, and instead it seemed that dog and man had entered identical states of connection to their surroundings, maintained not by control but by concentration of senses.

One day in late May, a bunch of us went with Bill out to Great Spoon, a nesting island a mile or so off the eastern shore, which the eider ducks share uneasily with the gulls. It's an unusual high island, rising from the cobble beach of the cove on the northern end to one-hundred-foot cliffs which extend halfway down the western shore and face the eastern shore of the Island across an archipelago of ledges and bare islets. Most of its rockiness is softened, particularly at this time of year, by a thick carpet of bright green turf with patches of wildflowers. Down deep in the grass, when we went out that time, there were strawberry blooms, and when we returned in the summer we spent a full half hour on our bellies in the grass at the windy top of the cliff eating those strawberries which we hadn't already crushed with our bodies.

Thanks to the human acquisition of all that nice down, eiders are a threatened species, and it's illegal to take their eggs; not so with gull eggs, and some of the islanders talk about having gone to Great Spoon as recently as several years ago for this purpose. In order to make sure that the gull eggs were fresh, they would make a preliminary trip to locate the gull nests, mark them and throw out the eggs they contained, returning the next day to gather the fresh eggs which the gulls had laid in the meantime. Nobody seems to do this any more, I don't quite know why. We gathered some gull eggs in the hope that they would prove to be fairly fresh, but we put them in Julie's fur hat and somebody stepped on them; they weren't all that fresh, but their yolks were nice and thick and yellow.

At nesting time on an island like Great Spoon, the gulls are the natural enemies of the eiders, as they will eat the eggs and the ensuing chicks if they are left unguarded. Bill had warned us to avoid scaring up the nesting ducks and to cover the nests of those we did with grass, as otherwise their locations would be revealed to the gulls who were waiting all around. As it was, we found that we were coming across too many nests down by the shore, so we moved to higher ground, and finally, feeling like clumsy invaders of a delicate environment, we stayed still altogether.

The deer are all over the place. The basis of their diet is the evergreen leaf of the cedar, but they eat other coniferous leaves and certain types of seaweed. They will also eat any kind of cultivated crop, and so every garden has a high wire fence around it—down to flower boxes, which are generally completely enclosed in wire. The fences have to be strong and high, as deer have been seen to amble up to one six feet tall and clear it with a standing high jump, and bucks have also been known to work away at less than the strongest wire fence until there is a hole big enough for them to go through. Their favorite food is apples, and at daybreak on September mornings there will be several wandering about among the houses in town, and it's not unusual to see one or two in town in the middle of the day. Often on winter nights, when I went out to the well, there would be a couple of startling snorts out of the darkness, and a couple of deer would bound off into the woods.

The entire deer population is descended from the two who were brought on in the 1880s to provide meat during the winters. In the ensuing years they have increased as they have interbred, and some people have told me that they have noticed that the individuals are smaller in stature than their mainland cousins. A naturalist I know has told me that a certain amount of work has been done on this island syndrome, and that the evidence leads to the conclusion that individuals of many species become smaller after generations of island living. It is not certain whether this is from a nutritional lack or because the absence of predators allows the weaker individuals to live and breed instead of being selected out, as they would be in an unisolated environment.

Although there are certainly a lot of deer, Bill feels that the population has a fair way to go before it reaches that critical size where it cannot feed itself and suddenly collapses. Many were killed in the severe winter of '70–'71, and, although no deer hunting had been allowed on the Island for many years, there is a fair amount of poaching, particularly in October, right before the meat toughens up during the rutting season. People from the Main and the nearby islands coast along the deserted southern shore in the fall, shoot a deer and then land in a small boat to pick it up. The problem with this is that if the deer is merely wounded they can't get to it in time, and it crawls off to die somewhere. It is nearly impossible to enforce the law when the hunting is from the water and so the poaching is pretty brazen—brazen, that is, by the standards of the Maine coast. There is a kind of black market for illegal venison on the Main, known as the "meat market," and most of its produce comes from the Island.

The past is held lightly by the Island. Its evidence is all around, in names, in houses, in old tools scattered about; and it merges casually with the present.

A couple of years ago Virginia MacDonald, the librarian, tried to get people to write up the histories of their houses and their families or reminiscences of former islanders. Some of the summer people responded—one or two doing very responsible jobs of historical research—and a couple of the older islanders rather enjoy an hour or two of reminiscence, but generally there is none of the historical-society fervor you would find in other places with such a long, rich past. As a matter of fact, there is just one historical account of the Island, apart from brief résumés at the beginnings of censuses, etc., and that one is a mere chapter in a casual book of reminiscences about the bay.

Leon Small, who died in Florida the winter I was living near his old house in Rich's Cove, wrote in response to Virginia's request that he didn't know for sure the building date and original owner of the house but that he thought the first to live in it was "a man known as Master Tyler who taught school on the east side. When he moved out, my grandfather Small moved in." Speaking of our mutual neighbor's house, he said: "The house Maurice lives in was taken apart and hauled with oxen by my grandfather Eaton and put together again where it now sits. The cellar that it came from is about halfway down the pond between the road and the ocean." He was talking about the mid-nineteenth century. Just think of the historical specifics: oxen hauling a house—Master Tyler and the drone of young scholars of the 1840s coming from a schoolhouse which still stands.

This is part of the deep past, but Leon Small lived in the house when he de-scribed it for Virginia, and most likely he went by the schoolhouse at least once every other day. He built the house we lived in all winter, and all summer we sat in the porch chairs which he ingeniously fashioned out of driftwood. He was casual; things last in fact, or are somehow perpetuated in kind down through the generations—no need to worry.

There are ten small cemeteries scattered over the Island, most of them so tucked away in little groves and corners that they're quite hard to find, even if you know their general locations. Sometimes it is as if people had been buried where they dropped. The names are the same as those still here or recently departed—Turner, Barter, Robinson, Rich, Hamilton, Small—and the dates go back 175 years. Often there are little bouquets of plastic flowers amid the real grass, real leaves and real flowers. This bothered me at first, but after a time spent among the pretty spectacular natural wonders of the Island, I began to think of these colorful little bits of fakery as evidence of *human* memory and concern, man-made outposts of resistance to the leveling of natural decay and to the impersonal strength of the sea, which is never far off. Also, the plastic flowers would last—a consideration not based on stinginess but on the knowledge that a trip to the grave to replace the decorations would involve an embarrassing display of feeling.

Pretty clearly, the Indians were on the Island first. The islands of Maine were generally used as summer camps by the tribes near the coast, and they came to this one to dig clams and hold feasts, leaving the shells in great heaps which, due to the permanence of the material, have lasted to this time, There are many of these on Kimball's Island, one of the satellites. Indians also drove ducks into the narrow head of what is now called Duck Harbor and killed them for food and feathers. After what I like to think of as a summer of relaxed hunting, gathering, eating, lying around and telling stories and making love on the soft forest cover (perhaps like one of those romantic sixteenth-century illustrations of the European concept of New World Indians) they would return to the interior of the Maine woods for the long, hard winter.

Indians continued to come occasionally to the Island from their reservations inland, and practically everyone over the age of thirty has memories of them. They came to gather sweetgrass for baskets or to sell the baskets they had made from the grass gathered the previous summer. I was told that, as recently as fifty years ago, they would spend the summers near the foot of the pond, camping with the permission of the landowner, shooting gulls (which was then legal) for the feathers and gathering sweetgrass.

Verrazano, in the sixteenth century, probably admired the Island; Champlain in the first decade of the seventeenth certainly did. There is a deep cove on the west coast which has a narrow and shallow entrance which can't be used at low tide; it's called Seal Trap now, but on a survey map drawn in 1803, the name is spelled *Ciel Trap*. The obvious conclusion, not original to me, is that some poetic Frenchman in a ship's boat came from the agitated waters off what is aptly named Trial Point through the tiny passage into the tranquillity of the cove, stopped there for a while (days? weeks?) and admired

The house on Burnt Island where Alice Crowell was born

the reflection of the sky, trapped in the calm waters. It is still admirable.

In 1772, according to one account, a man named Seth Webb, who had been living with the Indians nearby, got a crown grant for Kimball's Island, just across the Thoroughfare from the main island. The Island's interior hadn't been explored by then, as indicated by a beautiful map, published "by Act of Parliament" in 1776, which omits the pond just in from the west coast, a feature that wouldn't have been missed in anything but the most cursory exploration; this large area may have seemed forbidding and the small island more manageable. Anyway, the story has it that Seth Webb was killed by the explosion of his musket as he landed for the first time. His widow couldn't keep control of the island, and it was taken over by the Kimballs, who were wealthy and powerful.

Kimball's Island is inhabited by Jack and Alice Crowell, who live in the big farmhouse up the hill from the shore for all except the midwinter months, which they spend in a nearby city on the mainland. Alice was born on Burnt Island in the oldest unchanged house on the Island and its satellites, built in the first quarter of the nineteenth century. Her father was a captain and farmed the small island when he wasn't at sea.

To me, Jack Crowell has come to stand for all the master mariners I have never known (but always wanted to) who have retired to a house on a hill overlooking the sea. In the case of his house, the view is out over the town, but the Island is out to sea itself, so it's the same thing. Practically every day he rows the hundred yards over to town for the mail and groceries, and he and Alice are at every town gathering, but mostly we saw them through calls we made at Kimball's.

I had heard pieces of Jack's history from other people, and over the course of a few visits' worth of prying I think I got the highlights. Between 1926 and 1938 he made seven trips to the Arctic, as master of MacMillan's supply ships, and, understandably, became an Arctic expert. In 1941 he went to Greenland in charge of establishing the landing field at Thule which became the vital supply link to Russia at the beginning of the war. After being there several months he and his colleagues heard that Pearl Harbor had been attacked but were unable to get details because it was impossible to transmit. After the war he served in high positions on several Arctic trips for the Strategic Air Command and the National Science Foundation. Retired, he came back to the Island with the intention of fishing but says he found out, after a few unsuccessful attempts, that he didn't have the talent for it. That says a good deal about the business of fishing.

Peletiah and Henry Barter came in 1792 to the Island proper. It's reasonable to suppose, as has been told me as a fact, that they were veterans of the Revolution, who had been given grants by the Commonwealth of Massachusetts in gratitude for their services. The names of those who came immediately after the Barters were also English: Robinson, Kimball, Leland, Sawyer, Kempton, Smith, Turner, and so on; a Scot, Douglas, settled on the east side, and his land reverted to his son-in-law, Jonathan Rich, after his death. There are still Robinsons, Turners, Riches and Barters on the Island, and there have been similar English and Scots names, as well as an Irish, a Dutch and a couple of French (Huguenot) ones. It's hardly a melting pot, and the homogeneity shows best in the English faces of the school kids.

The Island schoolchildren

By 1800, according to one source, there were fifty settlers, of whom five were deep-water shipmasters. What the others were I haven't discovered; certainly they weren't full-time fishermen, as fishing didn't constitute a cash crop then. One, Calvin Turner, is said to have operated a salt works at Seal Trap, boiling the salt out of the water which had trapped the sky for the French two hundred years before, and this he must have sold for cash. Most probably, they farmed and fished for their subsistence. I'd suspect that they were different from the people of Massachusetts proper, as there seems to me to be an aura of old aristocracy hiding in the background of the Maine coast. Sir Ferdinando Gorges, who, in 1607, received a crown grant for the area which is now roughly Maine, was Anglican, as were his descendants who inherited the area, and he was therefore in conflict with the traditional Puritanism of the Massachusetts Bay Colony. The Hamiltons, who lived with their eleven children fifty years ago in a small house on Duck Harbor, are said to have been directly descended from a certain Lord Hamilton. I shouldn't be surprised.

In 1801 "Peletiah Barter and others" petitioned the Massachusetts legislature for sale to them of the land they had settled. The Island was then, politically and administratively, part of the mainland town, but because of the seven-mile barrier of open water, it enjoyed none of the town services for which the town taxed it. As a further argument for separation, the petition characterizes the land as so poor that the Island wouldn't be any loss to the town—in fact, good riddance. On the other hand, the roster of Island names 170 years later leads one to believe that the settlers found something to keep them around. By then it was home, difficult in truth as well as in political pleading, but still manageable if a remote, unsympathetic government would let them go at it in their own way.

The petition resulted in a survey and sale "to the actual settlers aforesaid at a reasonable price under all circumstances such lots as they shall be several found to possess . . . reserving for public accommodation convenient and necessary landing places in the several harbors in said Island." I'm not sure that the islanders got exactly what they wanted as a result of the 1801 petition, as they weren't set off from the Main until 1874 and so had to continue paying taxes to a political entity which was doing nothing for them. There is nothing like seven miles of open water to produce massive apathy in legislative halls when it comes to responding to the demands of a constituency. This, of course, is a political reality; islanders, because of geographical isolation, can't interact with other groups as easily as mainlanders can and form a confederation of interest to increase the pressure on lawmakers. Hence their interests tend to be forgotten. A couple of years ago one of the cities at the head of the bay, after two years of protest from its citizenry, decided to get the Army Engineers to remove the raw sewage from the bottom of its harbor, the sewage having become a threat (to say the least) to the clam beds and also having built up to the degree that it was a soft but real hazard to navigation. There was the problem of where to dump the stuff within what the Department of Interior gracefully called "the fifty-mile range of cost-haulage effectiveness," a problem which was solved by the choice of a site a good long way away from the complaining city but about five miles south of the Island. As the water in Moore's Harbor turned brown, and the fishermen began to speculate on what was happening to the lobsters around the Island, Ted Hoskins, the summer minister and an old resident, took the complaint to Senator Margaret Smith. As he said, it was too late, but at least the mainland knew at last that there was somebody out here.

By 1824 there were 36 deeded lots varying in size from 34 to 182 acres; most had what we now call shore frontage, but five large pieces were land-locked on the sides and top of the bare mountain ridge. Sixty percent of the total land was used, and what impresses me, looking at the survey map of that time, is how many areas which I now know to be wild are divided up with the kind of complicated boundaries that imply fences or stone walls sur-rounding and dividing fields. Assuming that each of the lots contained a family of five, there were about 180 people. There is no indication of a town or even a central cluster of houses. The names of those who arrived after the original settlers are just as English as before: Knowlton, Holmes, Wilson Merrithew, Harris, Gilbert—and Nathan Hipe, a name so deep in the past of England that it can't be found in the present Manhattan phone book.

It is not entirely clear what these people did. Certainly, if there were five deep-water shipmasters out of fifty settlers in 1800, there must have been some captains twenty years later. In 1900 there were a thousand sheep running over the Island, which implies that sheep had been grazed for some time. The safest general guess is that there was a good deal of subsistence animal raising, small farming and fishing; people spent the spring, summer and fall laying by for the hard winter, which surely would isolate them from a mainland which wasn't all that accessible at any time of the year.

There are hints that the Island wasn't completely isolated from the spirit of expansion that was going on then throughout the country. Calvin Turner called the sixty-five-foot schooner which he built in 1830 *Accumulator,* and I can only think that he named her in honor of the accumulation of money. She carried lumber to Boston, granite from the nearby quarry on the Main, kiln wood (the hardwood used to make charcoal) and probably a great deal else. There is a story that one of her Turner masters set out from Boston on the return trip to the Island one February morning alone, his one-man crew having shown up drunk once too often. He was in too much of a hurry, and I suppose in too much of a rage, to check his provisions, and he made the three-day solo voyage subsisting on rum and hardtack; when hungry he ate the hardtack, when cold he drank the rum.

It is reported that during the Gold Rush of the 1840s several families built a schooner in the Thoroughfare and sailed her around the Horn to San Francisco. (This report is from the same source that gives the Island population "at one time" as eight hundred, a figure which is generally doubted, so I don't know.)

One gets the idea of great activity from the old photographs of the Island's harbors made toward the end of the century. Being one of the outer islands, it lay in the natural course of vessels making the trip down east. It was accessible to the best fishing grounds, and in the days of sail accessibility was measured differently than it is now, when a boat can be started by a switch and moved fifteen miles out to sea in less than an hour. The Thoroughfare must have been filled with all kinds of craft in all but midwinter—schooners of all sizes used for fishing and freight; "traders," which were wide and shallow-draft, with a real house with doors and windows sitting high on the deck, filled with dry goods for sale to the various islands; lobster smacks with wells through which the sea circulated to keep the catch alive; and, everywhere the special small boat of the region, the peapod. This was a small double-ender which could be rowed or sailed and which was famous for its seaworthiness.

Clearly, at some point in the first half of the century fishing became the main business of the Island as well as a source of food. Before 1850 lobster had become a delicacy; at this point, I've heard said, you could gather lobsters at low tide in the tide pools, and you could certainly get your living from dipping them up out of the shallows or, later, by setting a few traps close to shore a lot more easily than you could fishing on the Banks or even from ground-fishing inshore. The ledge-filled waters around the Island were full of lobsters, as were most of the waters off the Maine coast. There was no need to go outside one's own immediate territory to haul a living, and a man could work within an easily established and easily held territory around his own port in the company of his neighbors.

Traveling cobbler, around the turn of the century

The Thoroughfare, at about the same time

In 1843 the first lobster cannery in this country was opened in Eastport, Maine, and in 1860 one was established on the Thoroughfare by a Boston firm. The process, which had been developed in Scotland, involved cooking the lobster meat and sealing it hermetically in cans. The Island factory at one time employed twenty-four people and sold the product to as distinguished and remote a customer as Crosse and Blackwell in London among others. Either at the same time or later, the lobster factory was used for packing fish in salt, which was stored next door in what is now a summer house. In 1880, which was ten years after the peak of the lobster boom, the factory closed. A minimum size limit was set in 1895, probably because people began to notice even then that the boundless resources of the wide sea were not so boundless as they had thought, and the larger lobsters brought more money when sold live than they did canned. The fishery went on just as strong, however, the Island hauling in its own waters like all the other Maine communities. The catch was carried live in the wells of huge lobster smacks, sixty to a hundred feet long, which came directly to the Island from Boston and New York, carrying back as many as fifteen hundred lobsters in a trip. The fact that these vessels could make a round trip from the Island to New York in one week gives some idea of the magnitude of this commerce.

In 1880 the population was 274, and in 1890 it was 206.

I gather that things were mostly carried around by oxen, and that the roads were no better than was necessary for this. There must have been some who had horses and even buggies before the summer people first came, but I gather that people walked most of the time that they didn't have too much to carry. The present road around the Island didn't exist, but there was a well-traveled trail over the mountain to the town—which by then had developed—from Head Harbor, four miles away on the opposite end of the island, and there was enough traffic on this path to support an ice-cream parlor located on it rather than on the main road of town. The path and the site of the confectionery have been lost in the trees which have grown up since.

In about 1880 the first summer people arrived—a bunch of Boston bachelors who established themselves as a club and began the development of the complex known as the Point. There had been no summer visitors since the Indians, and the islanders must not have felt an urgent need for prosperity in the form of tourism, so I would gather that they were merely tolerated. There had been an entrepreneur, one Colonel Montgomery, on the Island the year before, who had built a wharf and a dancing pavilion (expecting God knows what to happen), and conned the Island out of eighteen months of free board and lodging, the deeds to one hundred acres of land and sixteen hundred dollars in cash before vanishing into the West. People had just begun to discover that the Maine coast was one of the most beautiful places in the world and responded by imposing bulk, in the form of nineteenth-century "cottage" architecture, on the natural magnificence; Bar Harbor was just starting, for example, and in 1886, an entrepreneur from there, one Edwin des Isle (pretty funny-sounding name, if you ask me), came to the Island and built a hotel on the east side. He also built a brochure:

TOURISTS HOME

Realization of Quietude
A Resort for Recuperation Rest and Pleasure

A Fairy Land of Enchantment
Dreams of Romance Realized

Nature's Wonders
Unsullied by Man

The Hotel Des Isle burned to the ground two summers later; there used to be a story that Des Isle and his partner had fallen out and that one of them had set the fire. Considering the style of the brochure, I can't imagine that they fitted in very well; we present summer visitors try to keep our ecstasy in check.

In 1900 Clarence Turner was fifty years old. He was postmaster, kept a cow, pig and chickens, cut ice on the pond in the winter, built and repaired boats, built houses every once in a while, ran a livery for the summer people and, probably a little but not much later, strung wires all over the west side to the eleven points of an internal telephone system operated by the Point. He had a full life, but not all that much more so than many others on the Island. In nearly all the photographs I've seen from that time the men are wearing neckties; they may have put them on specially, but they also have a look of formal substance—of a self-assurance which then went with neckties.

A census was made in 1910, which gives the impression of a very lively place. The Island was probably no livelier then than at any other point since the end of the Civil War, but there are statistics and so the picture is clear. There were 178 people living on the Island year round that year. There were 15 summer families listed, containing 33 individuals as far as I can tell, all but one of these families living at the Point. Thirty-five families were supported by fishing—primarily lobstering by then—with a total of 46 listed in this occupation; in other words, there were probably 35 boats of various sizes going

A group of young men from the Island, around 1900

out from the Island, more than half of them handled by one man. Only 20 children whose parents lived on the Island had moved off when they had grown up and were living elsewhere. Twenty-nine pupils studied in the Island's two schools, and three students were off-island at institutions of higher learning.

There were two boardinghouses, one on Kimball's Island for summer visitors and one on the main island, which would accommodate guests the year round. Clarence Turner, as I've already mentioned, ran a livery and was a contractor and builder. There were three general stores on the Island and a barbershop-confectionery run by J. C. Turner, who was also a photographer and probably responsible for the old photographs reproduced in this book, although I can't be sure, as they are unidentified. There were two post offices, one in town and one at the Point, as there still are. Mrs. Myrtie A. Pettee ran an art store, which also sold fancy work and toilet goods. Haskell Turner was the blacksmith and made ornamental ironwork (some of which was exhibited in the Chicago World's Fair of 1893), and Willis Coombs had a carpentry shop. The library and the church were in existence, both operating only in the summer.

24   The census carries a list of individual occupations as distinct from the above

businesses. It includes a mariner (who went to sea in other than fishing
vessels), the captain of the mailboat (which also carried passengers, as it does
now), a part-time mail carrier who carried the mail from the boat to the post
office, two teamsters, the keeper of the lighthouse, one part-time machinist, a
farmer who grew wheat on Kimball's Island and hauled it across the bar to
the main island at low tide and a musician (why not?). The census doesn't
show how many people farmed on the side, but I gather that there were a good
many cows, pigs, chickens and sheep, and that nearly everyone had a vegetable
garden. Self-sufficiency was as necessary as it had been a hundred years before.

During the First World War, the population was 133, according to a newspaper article which reports that the town established a world record by having
a 100 percent membership in the Red Cross.

There has been a slow but steady decline in population since then. Skeet
MacDonald remembers forty fishermen who were here when he came to the
Island in 1921 and who have left since. There has been some immigration,
but there has been a net loss. In 1935 there were seventy-five winter residents,
and the number has been steadily decreasing to where it is now.

The State of Maine is among the poorest in the country, but I don't have the
impression that those who stuck it out on the Island were poorer than the
mainland residents. Some seem to have been fairly well-off. Clarence Turner,
who ran the livery and contracting business, died in 1952, and the list of
effects auctioned off includes as a partial list:

Burled Walnut Ship Captain's Liquor Case with Steigle Decanters, Burroughs
Adding Machine, Portable Smith Corona Typewriter, Servel Gas Refrigerator,
Washing Machine, Ford Truck, Antique Ford with Brass Radiator, Organ,
Twelve-Room Year-Round House with bath and electricity, a large two-story
Barn-Garage suited to store twelve cars, a large Three-Story building on water front
with a fine Wharf or Pier formerly used as a Canning Factory, approximately
75 acres, a 26 foot Motor Boat, and 18 foot Motor Boat and three row boats.

I was told that, in the middle of the Depression, one of the year-round islanders
asked the advice of a financier summer resident about the $100,000 he had
saved up and didn't know what to do with. I doubt that there were many
people on the mainland then who had anywhere near that amount, let alone
didn't know what to do with it.

The major reason for the decline in population is that it has become harder
to make money fishing from the Island than fishing from the Main. The Island
lobsterman's original advantage in being closer to the best lobstering bottom
has been canceled by the high-powered marine engines which everyone uses

L. C. Turner's house, now a summer residence

and which can carry a lobster boat from the Main to the waters adjacent to the Island in a matter of minutes. The dealers are on the Main and so it takes an extra round trip to sell, get supplied and get repaired. Food naturally costs more on the Island, whether the Island store has to add on the expense of transportation or whether the individual has to spend the time and/or gasoline to get it from the Main. As the fishing population has diminished, there is less of a fleet to maintain the sanctity of territory which was traditionally, if extra-legally, held by the Island lobstermen, and lobstermen from the Main have moved into water which their fathers stayed away from as being reserved for the Island.

There are no telephones, although nearly everyone has a Citizens Band radio. There are no movies and no restaurants. The list of inconveniences which make living on the Island difficult is so long that you begin to wonder why the population decline hasn't been more rapid. I guess that why it hasn't is the basic subject of this book.

2

ISLANDNESS

In 1902, Willard H. Palmer, a divinity student, came to the Island to serve as summer minister. He kept a diary:

June 21: I was brought here this morning, that is to the home of Mrs. Robinson where I am to live for the summer—Mrs. R. . . . did not give me a very hearty welcome this morning but then she does not know how to be really cordial. I think she is a kind hearted woman and I trust we will get on well together. She has a decided dialect, I suppose it is the Maine dialect. This evening at supper she talked about "chimbleys."

A month later:

Sunday evening July 6: I am not pleased with my work today—I wish I knew what the people on the island think of me. I suppose it is a blessing I do not know. It would probably take away my courage—

I had spent four summers as a child and about ten as an adult on the Maine coast before I came to the Island, and I'd illustrated a couple of books about the intertidal world. In short, I felt pretty familiar with the area; in truth, I *was* a lot more familiar than young Mr. Palmer—at least I knew what a Maine accent was, even though I sometimes still have trouble deciphering it. Nonetheless, when I read his diary near the end of my year of regular visits, the July 6 entry sounded familiar, and I looked in my notebook and found that in May I'd written the following:

Mystery: what do I really mean to the Island?—a winter diversion?— the Inspector General?—are people waiting for me to call?

Both Palmer and I, of course, had stumbled into a community. I don't know about him, but I know that Julie and I had never lived in one before; we thought we had, but what we'd lived in was a neighborhood, not a community. In the West Village area of New York, which we harked back to, we knew all of the storekeepers on, maybe, the two blocks around us, and when we went out on the street the chances were about fifty-fifty that we'd meet someone we knew; our son Mike, who was then a baby, waved out the window at the truck drivers at the warehouse across the street. It was nice.

A community is more like a family, and it isn't always nice. As a matter of fact, living in a family can be steadily miserable for days, months and some-times years. Always, it makes necessary the hard work of maintaining a mini-mum privacy in the face of physical proximity to the neighbors; this, in turn, involves getting along with yourself and/or your spouse well enough to make constant diversion unnecessary. It makes necessary the suppression of feelings which are so strong that to suppress them is downright dehumanizing—because how can you live in a family with someone you can't get along with at all? It makes necessary a concern with diplomatic minutiae which can make the court of Louis XIV seem like a barroom brawl. It makes necessary the subtle restraint of keeping a close friendship from becoming a divisive clique. It makes necessary a kind of basic good will and gregariousness which can make all of the above restraints bearable.

If a community is more than a neighborhood, it is also different from a com-mune. Unlike those in a commune, people in a community have separate houses, and there is a better chance for privacy, for a relief from the demands of getting along. On the other hand, a commune has a stated, formal purpose to help hold it together; to all intents and purposes, the Island is a collection of individuals with differing personalities and purposes. If someone wants to leave, there is no stated ethic of communality to deter him. It would be unthinkable for anyone to try to dissuade him from leaving, using the good of the community as an argument. The kind of obvious common endeavor which would be second nature for a commune just doesn't happen. A community garden was started in the summer, under the general ethic that you should work as much as you want and take as much as you want, letting your conscience be your guide; only Pat and Annie Haynes, the teachers, and a few of us summer types went near the place. Maybe, in an environment which demands constant attention to community, one wants a vacation from communal jobs unless they are absolutely necessary. And yet, when the summer people return and ask how the winter was, meaning first of all the weather, people say *we* had a good or a bad winter, *we* meaning the Island, long before they start telling about their own pleasures and pains.

Traditionally, islands have attracted special types. Of course, year-round residents have a much deeper commitment than the summer people, and they are forced to reaffirm this commitment often in some pretty dark times, but the initial attraction to the place is common to both groups, and this attraction could be called a longing for community. The longing exists apart from its having been tested, up to a point, and so one can speak of the recent arrival, the summer visitor and one whose roots on the Island go back 150 years in the same breath.

The rewards of living on the Island are complex. The one which might come to mind first is negative—living in a small isolated community is a way of avoiding the competition of the larger world, a refuge from real or expected failure. In some cases this might well be an important factor in coming in the first place, but it wouldn't be enough to sustain a permanent stay. I think it would be much easier to drop out in the middle of New York. I'm saying, by that, a little more than that each of us makes his own environment no matter what our physical or geographical surroundings are; to live on the Island is to live in a complicated environment which must be paid attention to. Indeed, the Island's social complexity is infinite, because if you assume that all individuals are infinitely complex, as I do, you can never totally understand a social unit which involves so direct an interaction among individuals as this one does.

Apart from the restraints I've talked about as taking up one's energy, the needs of the community draw you in, almost whether you want to be drawn in or not. This is why our neighbor in Rich's Cove, Gene Skolnikoff, comes here in the summer—not to get away from the telephone and the enormous pressures of an academic life although that is important, not so much to live in the physical beauty of the Island, but mostly to jump right into the middle of living among people who have chosen to live together the year round and who are pretty constantly reaffirming that decision. He explains that he would tend to avoid community concerns on vacation, as a rest from the committee work which is so much a part of his job, but here he can't help getting involved. Indeed, he was deeply drawn in. And it's not so much that the Island is a *different* place with a different kind of people as much as it's a community and that is a hard thing to come by right now in this country.

Bill Kirk, who is a summer *type* but on the Island a lot and deeply connected to it, has an expression, "out of time," which he uses to describe the place and his friends and neighbors here. At first I thought it was more or less a general superlative, a vague expression of love, but then I realized that it was an exact description of the Island as a place in which the *timeliness* of anything or anybody didn't matter. Wynne Skolnikoff, Gene's wife, speaks of the enormous variety which exists within the tightly bounded environment, a variety which can be seen clearly because the physical environment is so limited. Where else could she have been given a lift, as she was walking along the road a few years ago, by a really nice, formally dressed old gentleman in an antique car with brass headlamps. She said that, riding along next to him, she had to look down at her bare legs to make sure that she wasn't wearing a long white linen dress and the white, heeled shoes of 1919. She had lost the strict reference points which would have bound her life away from the Island; she hadn't returned to the past as much as she was living in an environment which was so strong that it could enclose several times at once.

All of this happens differently than it would on the mainland. The fact of isolation by water works two ways: the physical bounds make it necessary for people to form this kind of deep community and it selects out those who come here for all kinds of reasons, positive and negative, but who can't stand it. Also, the Island and the experience of living in its community changes people. I look back on my summer friends there who come from roughly the same background as I do, and I know that they're not much different from the people I associate with most of the time. Skolnikoff is hardly an old English name, and yet Gene is very deeply a part of the Island community and therefore completely different in my mind from those of his colleagues at MIT and Harvard whom I happen to know and who, when I come to think about it, are actually much like him. In other words, Gene and Wynne are other than the nice intellectual people we met this last summer in a nice place, as they would be, say, if we'd met on Martha's Vineyard. There, we might have talked about our winter— that is to say, *real*—lives, within the *background* of living in the summer place. Here, on the Island, I'd guess that nearly ninety percent of our conversation had to do with the Island. The relationship is reminiscent of shipboard friendships, which are traditionally dependent on isolation within a pervasive environment and are supposed to collapse when the outer world at the end of the gangplank is reached. But the concerns of the Island are deeper and more interesting than whether there's going to be Bingo in the lounge tonight, even though the environments seem to be equally isolating. When you meet

the shipboard friend later, you have to start off afresh, because in the cold light
of the outside world the life of the ship isn't very important. But the Island
is so absorbing and so important that I suspect that we and our friends there
will be fellow Islanders to each other in any circumstances. The circumstances
—New York, for instance—would be mutually strange to us rather than we
to the circumstances; it's as if we would always meet on the Island, even though
the Island was disguised as the place where we actually were.

The geographical fact of the Island makes a true community possible. Conversely, the community extends outward to include the physical island. Ted
Hoskins, who has been the summer minister for a number of years, taught school
the winter before last. Between fall and spring he stayed within the confines of
town; it was a severe winter, but not so severe that he couldn't have gotten
around to some of the rest of the Island if he'd wanted to. The fact was that he
didn't feel the need, that just being within the community was being on the
Island. I would have gone nuts—or at least I think I would have—being a
photographer and needing the stimulation of different views. Ted had a window
in his house which faced northwest into the teeth of the coldest of the winds,
and this was all the visual reference he needed. The people and the community
were what were important to him. He said that he was a different person when
he was on the Island, having a different space around him—a space which he
and the community made, extending outward to the farthest shore.

The postmistress, Miss Lizzie, who has been staying pretty close to home
the last few years because of a couple of broken hips, checks the Island
out by having someone drive her around it in a car a couple of times each
summer, but otherwise she doesn't have what you'd call an intimate, steadily
renewed knowledge of the place; she didn't even know where Eban's Head
was, which was a shock to me as I rushed about trying to digest everything
that first fall. However, she doesn't need to renew her acquaintance with the
physical Island to know it; sitting in the post office, she must feel it as the
space around her, about which she is given interesting little tidbits of current
information by types like me blowing in on her but about which she knows
all she needs to know to call it—the *whole* Island—home.

Isolation is thought to be bad for a community, leading to ethnocentricity,
lack of awareness and general soft-headedness; I'm not sure. The Island sits
off by itself with a kind of self-confidence, waiting for people to come to it.
Far too many people came to it last summer in the form of day trippers,

whom the town, which has few public facilities, couldn't absorb, but most of the time it's like a deeply beautiful woman who can sit calmly and receive her admirers with the grace which comes from knowing that she is beautiful. I admit that that's the positive side of it, the negative being that she's smug and self-satisfied. Anyway, a number of people have noticed that, when you're away, you're "off-island," whether you're seven miles away in town on the mainland or in Europe. I get the feeling that the Island doesn't think of itself as isolated; first, the islanders can be pretty sure that anyone who's ever been there longs to be back at least once a week, wherever they may be, so they can be pretty sure they're the center of a lot of people's attention; second, there's a lot going on even in the middle of winter, what with keeping the community going. For two whole months I had no urge to read *The New York Times* and, at the end of a Democratic primary race about which I had thought myself passionate, I hardly watched the very moving convention on the television set I'd rented. I realize I was involved in making a book, but in ordinary circumstances I think I'd have acted the same way. I'm not particularly proud of this lack of concern with the world, but I'm certain that it wasn't a withdrawal either. It's just that there wasn't enough time to live actively on the Island and do much else. I haven't checked, but I'd bet that the people who move off find that they have a lot of time on their hands that they didn't think they would have.

One thing that comes with living within the tight enclosure of the Island is the power to affect the environment that one has, or one thinks one has. I'm sure this has brought a good many people on, just as has the need to withdraw from the struggle of "the outside world." What could be better than to live in a tiny cohesive community, where one person honestly concerned with the public good and clearly seeing what should be done can be heard to effect; what a relief from the general condition of political frustration! The truth, which becomes apparent after a while, is that the Island is a poor power base, just as it is a poor refuge. Its politics are as complex as the city's in many basic ways; the establishment is just as established and resistant when it resides in four people as it is when residing in thousands, and as much public stupidity can be committed as in the whole city of New York (which is saying a lot).

However, it is true that a single voice can at least be heard better, and this attracts, and has probably always attracted, a *public* type of person to the Island, just as it attracts (but generally fails to hold) the dropout. One way to describe this public type of person is that he wants power, which is really to say that he wants to live in a community over which he has a chance of exercising some control after an honest competition of ideas and will.

The other way you could describe him is to say that he yearns for public *responsibility,* that he wants to give and receive a minimum amount of protection. A place like this, by its isolation, demands from everyone a public responsibility, which almost inevitably leads to public power. These are the Island's terms, and they are well understood. When I came on alone in the fall, I started to wander over the back trails of the Island as naturally as I would have anyplace. It occurred to me that I might possibly fall and break a leg and so I carried the usual minimum precautions (whistle, matches and space blanket) and let it go at that. It became apparent that this wasn't good enough for my neighbors Maurice and Helen Barter, who wanted to know more or less where on the Island I was going. Would they have started out in the dark with flashlights to find me, if ever I hadn't returned before nightfall? I never had a chance to find out, but it was clear that I was on *their* Island, and they had a responsibility for me which they didn't want all that much and which I would never have asked them to assume. There was nothing that either party could do about it—that was just the way it was.

Once, I stopped off at the post office at around five o'clock of a September afternoon and mentioned to Miss Lizzie that I was going out to Western Head in the full expectation that I'd be back well before it became dark at about seven-thirty. Her dryly expressed shock made be change my plans to a shorter trip, but still I didn't drive back into town until after dark. Some inspiration made me do the right thing for once, and I stopped off to check in with her. She said she'd heard a few cars go by but hadn't heard mine. My car at that time had a pretty distinctive noise, but I wouldn't have thought she would recognize it, as I hadn't been around for long. I can only guess that, as I set out on my adventure, a kind of subconscious sense of Island responsibility had made her file the noise of my car away in her mind in order to check my return.

The islanders don't make a big thing of taking care of each other and the strangers in their midst; as a matter of fact, they'd just as soon nobody noticed they were paying any attention. Jim Wilson, who teaches at the University of Maine and so can get to his house on the Island on weekends throughout the year, set out in his small sailboat one day in May from the Main to sail down to Head Harbor. There was a pretty heavy northwest wind and heavy sea

34   that day, and, although he didn't know it, someone who saw him set out radioed Harold Turner on the Island. Harold and Noyes MacDonald drove to the northwestern end of the Island, watched Jim go by Burnt Island, then drove to Harold's house, watched him clear the foul water around York Island, then drove to a spot on the southern end of the Island overlooking Head Harbor and saw him into sheltered water. Then, without his having seen them, they left, and Jim didn't find out that they'd spent the afternoon taking care of him until Noyes casually told him much later.

Community responsibility is a habit. There is an old tradition that when a man's wife dies, and he is left alone without heirs who would take him in and too old to remarry, he moves in with a younger couple with whom he is congenial in exchange for the bequest of his property to them. A man will often make an arrangement with friends—sometimes in his will—to take care of his wife, should be predecease her, leaving them the money for her care and perhaps something else besides. This seems strange when you first hear about it—someone buying love and care or bequeathing his wife—but it is the kind of direct, straightforward arrangement which could only be made in a community of people who find it second nature to take care of each other.

The biggest ego trip I had on the Island all winter occurred when a group of college students came down to the Island in mid-February to stay at Head Harbor in a partially built cabin heated by one space heater. There was an infant with them, and the winds of justified disapproval murmured about the Island for a couple of days. They had said that they wanted to leave on Tuesday, and on Monday it started to snow hard. Harold Turner, who was then running the mailboat, asked me to help pick them up in my four-wheel-drive Scout, as the Scout could make it through the drifts which were rapidly forming. This was a simple request, requiring not much effort, but the rewards were enormous—I felt like a real Islander, having been asked to help take care of the innocent outsiders, and one of the kids even asked me politely how long I'd been living on the Island. I was about to try to hide my peculiar accent in the cadences of the Maine coast but decided I couldn't sustain it. I was some pleased though.

What kept Harold and Noyes from telling Jim Wilson that they had been watching out for him all afternoon is important. It wasn't nobility; that is to say they didn't hide their good deed out of a sense that the highest form of Christian charity is that which is performed in secret. They're just as concerned about getting the credit due them as anyone else. It's just that to have been standing there when Jim came in, yelling things like Oh boy, were we ever worried about you, etc., as I might easily have done, would have been *immodest.* The average State-of-Mainer will go into contortions to avoid what might be taken, by the wildest stretch of imagination, as braggadocio. This trait gets stronger as you approach the coast and reaches mammoth proportions out on the islands. On one level, what this is is an unwillingness to say what you think, because you might be caught wrong, and, even if you were right, you could be caught thinking that such a thing as your being right was possible. This is known in Maine as being pretty sure of yourself, and it ranks in the hierarchy of sins somewhere between hauling somebody else's lobster traps and first-degree murder. It's not really the result of a massive inferiority complex—there is probably the same range of self-confidence on the Maine coast as could be found elsewhere—but it is a definite style.

It probably has something to do with the sea, and the habit that the sea has of making man seem small, of reducing his pretensions to knowledge of it. Nobody has ever referred to a sea god on the Maine coast—the deity is the same old Judeo-Christian one and is not talked about much—but it's as if the sea were personified into a god force, vaguely benevolent, but whose most obvious characteristic is a malevolent delight in upsetting human pretension. Too definite a weather prediction can bring on a whole gale, and so you take care—like the former mailboat captain who, when asked by a tourist if he thought it would clear up, replied, "It always does." That last example is a matter of a style, which I've called elsewhere here "Maine cool," but it's based on a real belief that you must be humble in the face of the sea.

One November afternoon when I was still using the sixteen-foot Whaler to travel between the Island and the mainland, I was due to go back to New York, and the wind had been blowing hard out of the northwest for long enough to kick up a particularly strong and angry sea. I wanted to get home, but I guess that the main push was that I had set myself on a path of action (cleaning up the house, saying goodbye, taking the car to town and the Whaler to the Main, someone in the Cousins family driving me to the airport, plane to New York, and so on) that was hard to retreat from. At the post office I said goodbye to Miss Lizzie, who expressed surprise that I was going across in this sea, but I explained that I had confidence in the boat (which it was pretty clear she didn't share) and that I was pretty sure that I'd be all right. As I was about to set off, Russ Deveraux drove down to the dock and, struggling in the conflict between the Maine ethic of minding your own business and his own humanity, told me he didn't think I ought to go. He'd just come across from the Main in his boat, which was somewhat more sea-worthy than mine; and he was very specific: if my motor held up, I'd be O.K., going slowly, but if it conked out even temporarily I'd be a mile downwind in less than a minute and most likely on a rock. He asked me if I *had* to go. This was a good question, as of course I didn't have to; it was only that I was set to go, and a kind of innocent arrogance told me that my personal schedule was going to be enough to part the waves.

Anyway, I made it across all right, going dead slow, even though at one point the boat left the water *completely* as it went over the peak of a wave. I asked the storekeeper at the Main to radio the Island that I'd made it and went on my way. On the plane it suddenly hit me that I'd been downright insulting, not only to Russ, but to all my new friends in the empty-looking town, who were not in evidence but who had all been aware of my departure into the steel-bright winter afternoon. The way they put it was that to go out into a sea like that in a dory scoop like that was a damn-fool thing to do, but that it was my own business. The fact is that if I'd gotten into trouble it would have been they who would have had to go out after me, and that if I'd drowned they would have felt responsible. Therefore, they knew that I had made it *their* business.

Russ's advice to me not to make the trip across that day was stated as a non-rhetorical question: "You sure you have to go over today?" That's about as directly stated as advice gets; generally it goes something like: *"Well"* (emphasized and followed by a fairly long pause), ". . . I don't know as I'd want to [do whatever it is he knows you'd be an absolute idiot to do]." I wasn't totally familiar with this style when I contracted with Maurice Barter, my neighbor, to insulate the walls of the house we were going to live in all winter, so I took him literally when he said that, *well* . . . he didn't know much about it, but he wondered if I really wanted to use tarpaper strips loosely nailed to the outside logs, as I'd said I did. Probably, he said, he was all wrong, but didn't it seem to me that plastic sheets would be just as good, because (1) there probably wouldn't be storms so intense that plastic wouldn't do the job, (2) he didn't have enough tarpaper on hand, (3) tarpaper would be pretty difficult to put on, etc. etc. I figured that Maurice knew a lot of things I didn't know, but I'd been thinking about those tarpaper strips on the outside of the walls off and on for a couple of weeks. Maurice's arguments, particularly

stated in the way that they were, didn't seem to offset all of the weighty
conclusions I'd reached after all that heavy thinking about how I was going
to keep warm during the winter. What I didn't realize was that Maurice
knew how to do the job a lot better than his arguments would seem to indicate
and that I shouldn't expect the same elaborate brief I would get in the
same situation in New York. He'd argue with me but only up to a point,
because the argument by itself had no pleasure for him. He really didn't care
as much about winning as he did about my doing the right thing. He probably
would have given in if it hadn't suddenly dawned on me that he had been
keeping the winter wind out of houses all his adult life, and maybe he knew
something his arguments weren't expressing. His object was to get me
to do what he *knew* was the right thing for both our sakes but with as little
assertion of himself as possible. The plastic worked fine, particularly as
he didn't have to win an argument to get me to use it. All of this was modesty,
not shyness or anything like that; I'm almost certain that he argues with his
wife the same way.

What I mean when I talk about Maine modesty is modesty of *expression*.
The divinity student was bothered that "Mrs. R . . . did not give me a very
hearty welcome." She probably didn't, according to the standards of cordiality
he'd been raised with, but he was perceptive enough to feel that she was kind-
hearted. On the Island, it is not really proper to open up like a great flower
at the mere approach of a stranger, because you may have to close down in his
face when you get to know him better. One should reserve most of oneself at
first and let little bits out at a time, expecting the same from others. Of course,
it is possible to be cordial and still be reserved, and the people on the Island are
as friendly as you'd want. Direct expressions of affection are not to be expected,
however, and maybe that was what the student minister wanted from Mrs. R.
Ideas are sometimes stated directly, but feelings about the person in front of
you never in any but the most devious, understated ways. As a result of this
verbal restraint, the smile of an islander is something to behold—one is
enough to keep you going for a week. I think I have a habit of being over-
effusive with people I like whose style is slightly foreign to me, and, despite
the fact that I'm letting it all hang out here, there were many times I restrained
myself from acting like Zorba the Greek, which was the way I felt but which
wouldn't have gone down well.

I think I know what the student minister missed on his arrival—a welcoming
committee. Maybe he didn't expect a brass band, but he probably expected

someone to meet him at the landing or at least to be given the feeling that someone knew he was coming. Obviously, everybody knew he was coming, and they were most likely all watching him casually from inside their houses as he walked up to Mrs. R.'s, but it would have been considered downright pushy to acknowledge his arrival. This standard of behavior has loosened somewhat since 1902, as I guess all regional behavior has, now that there is so much more interchange between areas of the country, but when Pat and Annie Haynes arrived on the Island to assume their duties as schoolteachers, they found nobody to welcome them, and the house which had been assigned them was locked. They had to go to the bathroom, and so they went across the street, where they were welcomed graciously and set on the path which would get their house opened and them settled and ready for the next step into the social interior of the Island. People weren't being unfriendly; it was just up to them, the strangers, to make the first move. This would lead to a friendly response, which would be reciprocated, and so on, but it all had to happen step by step and not in one big sploosh.

Someone who should know told me that the islanders were "frightened" of outsiders whose purpose on the Island they didn't know. The verb surprised me; the student minister seems a lot more frightened than Mrs. R., and I myself was certainly worried, if not frightened, when I first came on. It would seem that the islanders hold all the cards, that the stranger in their midst is beholden to them for everything. I certainly always felt that at any time the Island could have easily stopped this book and could even now, as I'm finally writing and printing the photographs for it. I felt at first that, in a number of ways, *I* was asking *their* permission to stay on. As a result I was always straight about what the book was going to be (which, at first, I could best explain by saying what it was *not* going to be—i.e., an exposé) and, pretty soon, this candor allayed what I would call "guardedness" but certainly not "fear"; a set of ground rules was very subtly established, and I think we all became easier.

Through it all I have felt like a petitioning rather than a threatening presence, because I could always be stopped. But maybe the Island didn't know its own strength. Certainly, now that I think of it, nobody ever ambled up and asked me to explain myself, as they're supposed to do in rural American towns, and as they probably do in fact; the questions about the book were worked elaborately into casual conversations. This forbearance is the result of the advanced state of civilization along the Maine coast, a deep feeling

that the right of any man to go to hell in his own way is sacrosanct. This ethic
is held so deeply on the Island that people can miss the point at which the
man on the way to hell starts to carry them along with him. The Island sits
like a diamond in the navel of the bay and the people who live on it have been
ripped off in various ways over the years. They have almost always been
exploited by those whose connections with them were not firm, and whose
motives they did not question in time. Not being capable of vigilante protective-
ness—and knowing that they're not despite their occasional threats to the
contrary—they are vulnerable. Maybe one could call them *overcivilized.*

For example, it's very easy for an island community to fall into the habit of
handling its law-and-order problems by simply throwing the offender off the
island and not allowing him back; the courts are far away over the water, as
are the state cops, and this works out fine, as the problem has gone away. I get
the impression that this method of protection by exile hasn't been used as much
as one might think on the Island. Once, during my first summer, a wandering
youth was caught at night in the store with his hand in the till, and he was
told to get on the mailboat the next morning in lieu of prosecution, but this is
rare. On the contrary, the reverse has happened. I was told that the Island has
even been used a few times as a place of banishment—that an erring resident
would be more or less paroled by the court into the custody of his Island
neighbors. This procedure would impose a burden on the Island community,
it seems to me, and one might understand its reciprocating by sending an
off-island undesirable back into the general society he came from without
recourse to the law, but it doesn't seem to have worked this way. I think
the Island (if it can be said to have a basic identity, which, being a community,
it must have) has the patience to force banishment by withholding its affection;
this doesn't mean anything as dramatic as being "put in Coventry"; I mean
that, if people persisted in being merely polite, a person couldn't last more
than a month—any month but July and August, of course, and even then,
in the middle of summer diversions, it would take a thick skin.

Any evaluation of how friendly a group of people really is has to be tested
against its attitude toward other ethnic groups. I haven't gone into this deeply,
but I've noticed over the years that there seems to be less ethnic prejudice on
the coast of Maine than in regions of similar population density. One obvious
reason for this is that there are few groups other than the predominant one
around, but I think it's more than that. Perhaps people near the sea are more
connected to the outer world than similarly isolated inland populations; per-

haps it is simply that in a place like the Island the predominant group has been around for so long that it has acquired the ease of self-confidence which allows it to live alongside people of other groups. There's always that point at which the incoming group becomes a threat, but by the time that happens around here the group has become more Maine than ethnic. There's one town on the coast in whose streets, fifty years ago, you could hear as much Italian spoken as English, because the nearby quarry employed mostly Italian immigrants (including a few master stonecutters from Ferrara). There must have been some friction, but I've never heard much evidence of it, and by now the Italian community seems totally absorbed. There are a few Jewish summer visitors on the Island, and the one I spoke to about this had never encountered anti-Semitism from the islanders, although in the past there was a great deal of it within part of the summer population. It's interesting that the Island wasn't infected, and now I'd doubt that there is any expressed anti-Semitism summer or winter. There are no blacks on the Island, winter or summer, but I would guess that it would be a lot easier for a black family to come to the Island than to an all-white resort on the New Jersey coast, for example. There would be awkwardness, but it would be well-meaning awkwardness. Naturally, if *two* black families came, there would be the usual change in attitude, but I think people would make an effort.

Technically the system of Island communication is minimal. There is a story, hotly denied by some but reaffirmed by others, that one of the influential summer residents on the Island in the thirties successfully sabotaged a plan to bring telephone service to the Island, because he wanted to spend a month without the responsibilities which would have followed him on the telephone. The service would have been accomplished by a submarine cable or, later, by radio-telephone, and it would have been important to the morale of the Island in the middle of winter. At that time there was still in existence an intra-island phone system which connected the Point to the further reaches of its empire, and from the distance of the present it seems to have been a rather highhanded thing to do.

By now, there are too few potential year-round subscribers to justify a phone service, and so the Island makes do with Citizens Band radio, a special wavelength for short-distance transmission. This is a pretty common method of communication on the Maine coast. Listening in, you get the impression that the average fisherman gets up in the morning, eats breakfast in the usual silence, goes out to haul and immediately turns on the CB to chew over all the early-morning gossip, which by then his wife has also picked up on her set. This conversation is in code, of course, and if young Dr. Palmer thought he had a rough time with Mrs. R.'s accent he should be around now to hear what "chimbleys" sounds like filtered through radio static and the noise of a 150-horsepower marine engine.

On the Island, you could be pretty sure that, if you were doing anything noteworthy in public at about 7:30 A.M., it would get pretty good exposure, as, for example, when Pat Haynes shinnied up the school flagpole in his black motorcycle suit one cold winter morning to free the pulley on top so that the flag could be raised. There was talk. Elthea Turner speaks every morning to a man who lives alone on a nearby island, and she has never met him in all the years they've been doing this. There is the disadvantage that everyone who happens to be on the air hears every conversation, but this doesn't bother a close community which speaks in a code of meaning as well as a code of accent most of the time. The necessarily bland style of radio conversation, in which one has to say or indicate "over" after every thought, just puts another barrier in the way of the loose expression of thoughts which maybe should be chewed a bit longer anyway.

I don't understand the nontechnical, or real, method of communication as well as I'd like to, but I've been on the Island only the better part of a year. In the communication of relatively unimportant matters, such as a favor you'd like someone to do for you, it is usually only necessary to tell some one other person to have it reach the person you want it to reach. People stop and chat a little when they meet, so that pretty soon everyone has checked in with everyone else. On a superficial level, there isn't so much red-hot news happening that B would not remember when he's talking to C that he met A a while ago who happened to mention that his generator blew up and does C have a wrench? It's a little slower than the telephone but, surprisingly enough, not that much slower.

The communication of serious matters often works as follows: when A has been treated badly by C, he will complain to a third party, B, in such a direct, frank manner that it would be evident in any other society that B should keep it to himself. The complaint may go deep into the past and the offense may be great. B, in what would seem a betrayal of A's trust, will let C know of A's anger over the course of a great deal of time and in a great many references within a great many conversations about other things. Perhaps he will use B1, B2 and B3, but most of the time he will do the job himself. The objection to the offense has been registered, and C's explanation, if there is one—or anyway his position on the matter—is told to B and starts its long way back to A.

While all this communication of anger goes on through B, the disputants A and C are being downright friendly to each other, and of course B is friendly to both of them as being outside the dispute. This is not hypocrisy. It is the absolutely essential cushion to anger which makes it possible for people of great difference to accept and even enjoy each other despite differences. In any other place, A and C could avoid one another, as, for example, a divorced couple can live with ease separately in a small town. On the Island they cannot, and they know it. The islanders know that it is inevitable that they will make enemies as well as friends, and yet they stay in this place where—not as a matter of good will but as a matter of social necessity—they have to get on with people they have every reason to dislike and who may have equally good reasons to dislike them. This way of living could be called a number of things—hypocritical, provincial, unjust—but it could also be called highly civilized.

Actually, I even knew gratitude to go through a middleman; I got the feeling that the more gratitude was felt the more it was indirectly stated. There seems to be a premise that as long as feelings of love and hate cannot be expressed completely—as, indeed, they never can be anywhere—it's better to leave them inferred by not speaking than to speak inaccurately. I'm not that way; I tend to circle things passionately and close in on the heart of the matter noisily, and for that reason I'm probably remembered on the Island as a romantic. It was nice to be challenged by another style.

One result of this lack of confrontation is that the community develops a kind of subconscious which absorbs all the gossip, bitterness and affection which would otherwise have to be directly expressed. It is through this subconscious that an individual is elevated or demoted, and it is this subconscious, I think, which runs the Island.

The only formal expression of this governance is the annual town meeting, held traditionally on the last Monday in March. It has occurred to me that, since the Island really runs itself subconsciously, by understatement and nonstatement, the plain speaking which is supposed to be the heart of government by town meeting could easily impose a threat. However, I guess the truth is that what transpires at the meeting constitutes just one more *indirect* form of communication. The meeting forms the framework of ritual which can provide one method of settling problems.

On the face of it, the town is governed by a board of three selectmen. There are a town clerk and treasurer, a tax collector (to whom, for example, I paid the excise tax necessary for the registration of the old car I left on the Island) and a school board. There are three constables, a fire warden and chief and a secretary of civil defense. There are five other separate offices, the duties of which are assumed by the selectmen: road commissioner, overseers of poor, tax assessors, sealer of weights and measures and surveyor of wood and timber.

Almost sixty percent of individually held offices are filled by women. I'm not sure of any definite conclusions which can be drawn from this, but I noticed that there seemed to be a total lack of what we've come to call sexism, in that nobody seemed to be aware of the proportion. I began to wonder if the Island might not be a Utopia of integration of the sexes or whether this easy interrelationship might just extend to local government. On the other hand, I had no feeling that the men had abdicated their responsibilities in a kind of group contempt, such as one might find among fathers of schoolchildren loath to get involved in their P.T.A. because that is supposed to be woman's work. I felt that gender made absolutely no difference in the degree of respect shown any of the officers or anyone who got up to speak. Could this really be?

The town appropriated about twenty-four thousand dollars to run itself, about half of that being used to run the school. There is no town debt and there are no unpaid taxes, although the state allows a certain amount of town debt and most towns on the mainland think they're doing well if only twenty-four percent of taxes due remain unpaid.

The formal opening of the town meeting, familiar to all the islanders, quickly broke down into an orderly informality. The business of the first article was to choose a moderator. Someone was nominated, she demurred, and then she was asked formally: "Are you declining?"

"No, but I just hoped I wouldn't have to do it again this year."

She was elected. There was an easy movement in and out of formality, which I imagine comes from deep familiarity with and belief in parliamentary procedure. Once the moderator asked: "Did I say that right?" Article 13 asked the town to choose a surveyor of wood and lumber. Someone was nominated, and he replied: "You can go to hell—that is to say, I respectfully decline."

Out of the steady rhythm of consideration of noncontroversial business, matters of importance and issues involving conflict would come up. By my perhaps innocent count five of the articles precipitated oblique discussion of two issues in conflict. There had been a great deal of thinking and a certain amount of casual caucusing beforehand, arising from the general reluctance to bring something up at town meeting unless one feels it absolutely necessary to do so, and so everyone knew pretty well which articles and which conflicts these would be. At the appropriate times, the controversies rose gently to the surface, where, still half submerged, they would be poked at gingerly (or so it seemed to me). On the other hand, if the conflict had to do with a specific person, things would screech to a halt, and there would be a fairly long silence before the oblique, mildly stated argumentation began.

These arguments, of course, were in community code. I guess there was some resolution, but the solutions were hidden in a morass of inference which was indecipherable to me, a stranger. Most often, the matter would be pushed no further than absolutely necessary for minimum community requirements. At some early point one or more signals would indicate the sense of the meeting and the disputants would withdraw, allowing the issue to settle beneath the surface again. I noticed that it was very important that each conflict have the appearance of resolution and that someone would often add a kind of coda to soften the bitterness, so that the Island could get on with the business of living together.

The meeting had started at one o'clock and by four the level of extraneous noise indicated that it was about over. It had been a hard-working three hours for everyone; despite the informality and air of good humor (the little children wandering around, sometimes happy and sometimes complaining), people had paid close attention to the agenda. Mostly, I felt that everyone was tired from the effort of giving voice to abrasive concerns while remaining friendly and calm. The minutes were read and approved at the end of the meeting, indicating the real importance of what had transpired, and the officers were sworn in.

Mr. Palmer writes in his diary:

Fri. July 11: . . . This evening I went to the East Side to hold a meeting in the Schoolhouse. No audience came by eight o'clock so I left. On the way back I met some people on their way to the meeting. But I did not go back with them. Such sublime indifference to time is astonishing.

The Island does indeed seem to be on a different time scale. However, Mr. Palmer was wrong that there is an indifference to time; it was just *his* time they had lost track of. None of these people would have shown up at the shore more than a few minutes off a certain point in the ebbing of the tide, if they had wanted to dig some clams, or more than a few minutes from the full flood of the tide if they had to unload at a dock or get over a ledge. There is a basic rhythm to the day, and it is still pretty much a rhythm set by the two high and two low tides in every twenty-four-hour period. The tide is a rigorous and complicated factor in everyone's life. The times of the low and high tides change every twelve hours, and just how far out the tide goes and how far in it comes are constantly changing according to the phase of the moon. To a lobsterman the state of the tide at any one time has all kinds of consequences, the most obvious of which is whether he can get in close enough to a certain ledge to haul that particular string of traps, but it also means, for example, that a woman carrying a load of shopping from the Main has to climb a gangway gently angled at high tide at five degrees or angled for a mountain goat, at low tide, at fifty degrees. You could ask almost anyone on the Island when the next high or low water is going to be, and chances are they could tell you within a half hour. The tide times are absorbed in childhood, and once the interior clock is set going, it seems never to have to be wound or reset.

The day is partly governed by the predictable rhythms of the tide, but it is also governed by the highly unpredictable factor of the weather. Most of us in this country have gotten farther and farther from caring about the weather the more we have tried to overcome it, and it is quite an experience to have it determine things like whether you're going to work today or not, or whether or not you're going to get to the hospital on time when you're sick. Here in New York I didn't know it had been raining for most of the morning today and, when I found out, all it meant to me was that I took an umbrella when I went out. The combination of predictable tide and unpredictable weather (we can go at high water unless it's foggy; if the wind's from the northwest we can't land except at low water, when we can get in behind that big boulder) creates a continuously complicated set of conditions which cannot be affected by anyone. If you live with daily uncertainty, you adjust to it or go mad, and the way you adjust is to wait until the factors of tide and weather combine with man-controlled factors like the availability of materials, the smooth operation of a machine, health, and so on to produce what is known on the Maine coast as a *fair chance*. Always I heard that phrase: one has to wait for a fair chance to complete almost any job. Before the dock was built, passengers had to get onto the mailboat from a small boat which was launched from the beach below the schoolhouse in all kinds of sea conditions. Waves tend to come in threes, but you can't count on it absolutely, and so you would wait to throw yourself or your worldly goods or your Aunt Minnie into the heaving boat—now! The trick was to recognize the moment after waiting for it, because you couldn't *make* it happen.

After you've been waiting patiently for fair chances most of your life, you develop a pace which is infuriating to student ministers—and also to summer visitors who have to pack their Island experience into two weeks of vacation—but it is really the most *efficient* way to function within the natural complex. If you have a number of things to do in the next few days, most of them depending in part on the combination of tide and weather with a number of other factors, you will function best if you can decide easily at any one point, given any set of conditions, which job is impossible to do, which one merely difficult and which one easy. Therefore, you are always juggling a number of possibilities in the air, each waiting for its own fair chance of accomplishment.

This system doesn't slow life up, as there is always something to do; on the other hand it produces a kind of total awareness of the environment. It produces a pace which seems unambitious to those of us who have spent our lives under the shadow of the assumption that we can do anything at any time if we will only get down to it, but in truth it is a pace which is lively enough to be difficult to maintain. I ended up the summer with a list of places, people and events to photograph, each of them depending on a specific time, tide, weather or light condition for what I thought was their right moment. I don't like to work this way, but at that point the necessity for coverage took precedence over the freedom of photographic response. I made a list, to which I'd refer at any time I thought I had nothing to do because the conditions weren't right, and I'd generally find something for which the conditions *were* just right. Most people on the Island have just such a list in their minds; one activity leads to another as the day goes along, and the jobs gradually get done.

For example, one day in early spring it seemed to a few of us like a fair chance to try to clear the road around the Island of the trees which had fallen across it in a recent storm. There were about eight of us, men, women and a child, and we slapped together a picnic which we ate on the way. Was it work or an outing? Both and neither; it was a day on the Island. We were stopped by the soft snow on the southern end of the Island and had to turn back sooner than we'd expected. As we passed Pat Tully's house on the way into town, Harold van Doren asked to be let off, as he had some sawing to do at Pat's. He had the chain saw with him, he had a little time, he happened to be passing by, and so the job was done—easily, within the pattern of that particular day.

To a large extent, this pace, which comes from the organization of one's time to fit in with the governance of nature, is what is most precious to the people on the Island. It is this pace, also, which brings most of the summer people here, as a respite from the necessity to do such-and-such right now, according to a schedule set by men and maintained by men with a rigidity which cannot be affected by things like fog.

Willard Palmer, who sounds to me like a really nice person, ends his diary as follows:

Fri. Sept. 5—When I look back over my summer I don't know where the time has gone to—I have not gone fishing with the men as I intended and ought to have. I have planned to once or twice but the weather has prevented each time. For the last three weeks especially it has been very hard to work. There seems to be something about this island or the atmosphere which makes people sleepy. Others have spoken of it and I have felt it lately.

I would say that he had switched partway to Island time, like a transatlantic air passenger who can't quite catch up to his body after the time jump. The islanders weren't sleepy, as he thought, but just were in another state of concern. If you've arrived in the rarefied atmosphere of the center of things and haven't quite adjusted, you can easily feel sleepy.

In an article on Vance Packard's book *A Nation of Strangers,* James Reston pointed out that "forty-two million Americans change their home address at least once a year," that there is "a countermovement of young away from the cities, not into a settled life of countryside but into a life of constant movement." This it terrible—it's decivilizing. The community was where it all started, and if there are no communities left, if there is no one place whose scale you know and whose scale gives you your own scale, you may have a hard time of it. As Reston says, it's a common American problem, but I'm sad that I didn't know a place like the Island until I was forty-six.

3

TOOLS AND TECHNIQUES

The Island has a disposal problem—as, of course, all islands do, including the island-planet Earth. The usual waste is mostly taken care of by septic tanks and garbage pits and occasionally by dumping into the sea, which is illegal these days. Sometimes the Island receives material which it hasn't manufactured. There was the incident of the sludge carried from the harbor and dumped near the Island, which I've mentioned. Furthermore, one of the summer residents at the Point told me that every summer, inevitably, he will be standing around the dock there, and a girl in a bikini will come ashore off a half-million-dollar yacht, hand him her garbage, smile prettily and return to the boat.

Except for the plastic thrown out with the garbage all of the above is de-composed fairly quickly, but junk, unlike garbage and human waste, sticks around a bit longer. Jim Wilson got up one morning, looked out his window at the meadowland around his house at Head Harbor and realized, as he later told me, that he was living in the middle of a used-car lot—a *very*-used-car lot. In almost every direction there was at least one abandoned car sinking into the receptive earth. Maybe the sun was at just the right angle to cause lots of reflection off the decaying bodies or maybe Jim was depressed that day, because he hadn't noticed it before, and it didn't bother him too much afterward, being part of the expected condition of the Island—but just once he had seen the collection of derelict cars with blindingly objective clarity.

49

The first cars were brought over by barge around 1910, were driven and repaired until they fell apart and were dragged out of the way. Out of the way generally means to the side of the road, but sometimes cars in various stages of decay can be found in the middle of the woods, having gotten there on paths which by now have completely vanished. There is a story that an enterprising mainlander came on the Island a few years ago and stripped the prewar corpses of their antique parts, sometimes removing the whole bodies. What remains are the cars of the fifties and early sixties, which were so ugly when new that their looks improve as they disintegrate. If they haven't become one with the soil, to my eyes at least they don't dominate the land any more, and I don't mind them as much as most of my neighbors do. There is talk of hauling them off to a proper graveyard on the Island, if the land can be found, or to the Main, if the money to transport them can be raised. Harold van Doren would like to crush them into manageable packages, if he could get the necessary equipment.

I guess that part of the problem I have in sharing the common disgust at the junk cars is that it seems inconsistent with my love of the old tools and pieces of machinery which lie about all over the Island. The junk cars of the fifties are the visible remains of a technology which produced junk new, but in an earlier time things were made honestly with real material which, unlike plastic, is mortal. They were made well by craftsmen, and the tools were made for the use of craftsmen, and, rusting away, they evoke the lives of vigorous, intelligent people.

The intricate technology behind fishing and traveling about on the sea is absorbed by young boys, practiced, improved, refined and passed on easily to the next generation. Charles Turner, Harold's father, was an excellent navigator, as were all good fishermen then and as they are now. Harold remembers his father, one day of total fog when visibility was down to about ten yards, figuring a twenty-mile course from where they were on the other side of the bay to a buoy just south of the Island. He had to make the usual complicated adjustments for tidal drift and estimated that they would reach the buoy in two hours and fourteen minutes. Harold, who was at the wheel two hours and fourteen minutes later, cut the motor, the boat drifted under its own momentum for about thirty seconds, and the buoy came out of the fog twenty feet away. Evidently, it happened that way enough times to be more than luck. When the old man was eighty years old, he was out hauling with his sons in another thick-of-fog near the Island and gave the course to home. After running a while, one of the boys realized that they had gone right over Horseman's Ledge and had only missed it because the tide was high enough for the rock to miss their bottom by a matter of inches. He told his father and the old man never gave another course for the rest of his life. It occurred to me that under the same circumstances I would have been mortified and depressed and might have even claimed that I'd known all along that the tide was high enough to clear the ledge. Harold said that he didn't think his father felt more than a moment's irritation with himself—he just knew that it was time to quit. He knew, and his sons knew, that everything *they* knew about the sea, boat handling and fishing they had learned from him, and so it was easy to hand over the authority.

The inconvenience of getting things from the mainland has always meant that it is easier to repair than replace and that it is easier to do a job oneself than to wait for an expert to come out. As a result a tradition of innovation has developed. I got so used to expecting this ingenuity that, when I saw a sixty-year-old photograph of what turned out to be the chassis of a wagon being transported across the Thoroughfare in a boat, I just naturally assumed that some typical islander had attached wheels to the boat and had made the first amphibious peapod. It seemed like the kind of thing which had always been done and was still being done. For example, Russ Deveraux designed and built a trailer whose deck was at such an angle to the plane of the wheels that it could be let down the beach into the water and used as a dock for the unloading of groceries and then drawn up the beach, to whose incline it conformed, without spilling any of the load. Doug Heline was bothered by the rattle of a loose exhaust pipe running up through the cabin of a lobster boat he had borrowed while his own was being repaired. A rag or even a wedge of wood stuffed into the space between the pipe and the edge of the hole through which the pipe went wouldn't have worked because of the heat of the exhaust, and it would have been a bigger job to repair the ill fit than he would have wanted to undertake in a boat which was not his, so he attached a coping-saw blade to the deck near the pipe in such a way that its natural tension held the pipe firmly against the side of the hole and stopped it from rattling.

There is a kind of spare elegance to this simple solution of a problem by the use of what comes to hand. Many children are able to use castoff material to build fantasy constructions, but they lose this ability to improvise when they grow up and are supposed to make enough money to buy things new—particularly if they grow up in consumption-happy America. On an island, where improvisation is often the alternative to a time-consuming trip to the mainland, the art is preserved in the realities of adult life. At work is the same fresh imagination and, more important, the presumption that something not blessed by a manufacturer can work.

The ability to improvise comes in handy on the sea, where an emergency can come up so quickly and can take such unexpected forms that no amount of foresight and preparation can help. If, say, your motor conks out when you're close to the windward side of a ledge, you have only a short time to do *something* before you go on the ledge. Every situation is different, and a lot of the time the circumstances make it impossible to do what you might have anticipated you would do in that particular type of emergency. Once, long ago, Maurice Barter's boat let go of her mooring in a bad storm. He and an uncle of his were at the wharf when it happened, and, as the boat started toward the rocks at the head of the cove, they saw that it would come within twenty feet of them. As I reconstruct it, they had about forty-five seconds to pick up the nearest thing at hand, which happened to be a crank handle, tie on a line and throw it aboard the boat as it sailed by. By good chance it caught on the combing near the stern. As they were unable to launch a skiff, and as the boat was too heavy and the sea too severe to haul her in to them without the crank handle coming loose, they held her that way for eight hours until the storm abated, while Helen Barter brought them coffee. It takes a lifetime of experience with the sea and a lot of self-assurance to figure that you might even have an outside chance of getting away with something like that.

Nearly everyone on the Island knows a lot more about things like carpentry, plumbing, electricity, automobile mechanics and the like than people in similar occupations who live on the mainland, simply because they have to; it's always difficult and often impossible to get a specialist to take the time to come down to the Island for any one job. Aside from the amount of expertise that is picked up casually as a result, there is a good amount of downright studying that goes on. People get the literature and those who have a special knowledge share what they know. Combining this special knowledge with the general handiness of all good fishermen can produce a pretty able community, and a lot of things get done which are not supposed to get done without experts. Very quietly, Jack MacDonald, a fisherman, decided he just might be able to design and build his own house, just as quietly he set about studying how to do it and asking questions, and pretty soon he had a new house. A few members of the community—also amateurs—dropped in from time to time to help him—particularly Bob DeWitt, who works as a bishop when he's off-island. All the time Jack was building the house, he professed to be unsure of what he was doing, but I think that was just to ward off devils.

One of the most impressive acts of self-sufficiency in recent years is the establishment and maintenance through all kinds of struggle of the Island's electric power cooperative. Until two years ago individuals provided their own electricity by gasoline generators. Many of the summer people eschewed electricity as being unnecessary to their happiness and the noise of a generator as being an insult to the quiet of the evenings. They had gotten used to kerosene lamps—the ordinary kind and also Aladdin lamps, which make use of an incandescent wick and so give off about as much light as a sixty-watt bulb until you take your eyes off them for a second and the wick burns up. Propane lights, which give off a bright, harsh light, and candles are also used.

During July and August we lived in a house without electricity, and I expected that it would be difficult for ordinary evening life and impossible for any work after dark. Actually we liked it; the yellow light given off by the kerosene lamps was soft and beautiful and allowed the corners of a room to remain gently mysterious. If you wanted to read, you went through a chair-setting and wick-adjusting ceremony, and you glanced at the wick nervously every now and then, but I found it quite possible to do all my work except looking at pictures. In our bedroom there was a bureau with an enormous mirror, which, when reflecting a couple of kerosene lamps and three candles, turned the tiny space into a nineteenth-century ballroom. It became possible to feel the immediate presence of a quality of life which had vanished seventy years ago, as one prepared for the coming of evening by filling the lamps and cleaning the wicks, or when one looked at the house at night from outside. There was an unfamiliar acknowledgment of the darkness which is impossible with electricity. We pumped our water from the well to a storage tank on top of a ledge above the level of the house by means of a one-cylinder motor which I'd start up every time I got stuck in my writing, so we always had lots of water. The water was heated by propane, we had a battery-powered radio, and for two months we didn't miss the usual appliances too much.

On the other hand, this was summer. For half the year the darkness comes cold and early, and it would have been distinctly unromantic to be without electric light on a December evening, as December evenings start around 4 P.M. By the end of the sixties the difference in cost and convenience between running a family gasoline generator and paying for the ability to switch on locally generated power became too unreasonable a difference between living on the Island and living on the mainland seven miles away. The Island had to make an effort to close the gap for the sake of its life, as it might be this one factor which would make an essential family decide to leave. In 1970 there were a few opening moves toward the establishment of a power cooperative. Russ Deveraux, now the owner of the Island store, tried to get the Rural Electrification Administration's support, but Washington is just as far away from the Island as the seat of the Commonwealth of Massachusetts was in 1801, and it became evident that, as usual, the Island would have to take care of itself. Ted Hoskins delivered an exhortation one Sunday in church, there was a drive for subscribers among the winter and summer residents, and the power cooperative was established under the management of Pat Tully, who had also done a good deal of the work in getting it started.

Pat Tully is thirty-three and has been living on the Island full time for eight years after a childhood of summer residency. He went to prep school and college, and shortly before he graduated from architecture school he left and came to live on the Island. He lived alone for a couple of years and then married Donna Dodge, one of the daughters of Dotty and Stanley Dodge, Jr., who was then the captain of the mailboat. Pat and Donna went down to Jamaica for a week or so in the middle of the winter I was on, visiting his mother in what I imagine are fairly luxurious surroundings. When his mother died last spring they went down to Boston and stayed in the Beacon Street house to take care of various responsibilities, until it became time for Pat to get back to the Island to continue putting in the poles for the electric power and time for Donna to return to help Helen Barter clean and open up the summer cottages on the Point.

By the time I arrived on the Island, the electrification extended from the generating station near the town dock to the north end of town. The next step involved continuing the service down the east side for about four miles as far as the farm at the head of the pond. There would be a side line going down to the Point, as the association of summer members had decided to hook onto the power co-op after their present generator wears out, but this was a matter for the future. There was also Rich's Cove to electrify, but that too was off the main road and of lesser priority.

Pat, with the help of Harold Turner and Maurice Barter, concentrated on blasting the main line of post holes out of the solid ledge which most of the island is made of. From somewhere out of his past Harold had dug up a dynamiter's license and the knowledge to support it, so he was more or less in charge of this part of the operation; I say "more or less" because I doubt that there were any lines of authority, once Pat, as power company president, had decided that work would go ahead. Evidently, dynamite by itself is not as dangerous as I'd always imagined it to be; however, when the detonator cap is attached to a stick of it, it becomes tricky to handle, so the idea is to keep the two apart until the last moment. For that reason the dynamite and the detonators arrived on the Island in separate boats, Harold got Pat to memorize the list of safety precautions on the cover of the dynamite box, and they were ready to go.

I was on the other side of the Island when the first explosion went off, and that afternoon I went around to watch. First, they drilled holes into the solid ledge with a pneumatic drill which Pat had rented; the detonator caps were put on the dynamite sticks by Harold and passed to Pat, who put them into the drilled holes. The two cables from the detonator were strung out to about a hundred yards and, rather casually I thought, touched to each terminal of the battery of Pat's truck. I guess what I'd expected was that someone would yell "Timber" or at least "Watch it" or something; instead the dialogue went something like "Okay?"—"Guess so"—BOOM, and I never did get a picture of the moment of explosion, being too reticent to ask for a countdown. Maurice taught me the trick of looking at the rocks and boulders as they flew up a hundred feet in the air and watching for the one which didn't seem to move as it came down, as that would be the one coming straight toward you. The blasted hole would immediately fill with water from the many springs which go through the rock of the Island, and the next half hour would be spent getting it out with a portable gasoline pump and shoveling out the loose rocks.

What unmitigated gall for these guys to think they could handle dynamite! However, there was a set of circumstances to justify doing so. First of all, they knew that it would take more money than the power company had to get a dynamite crew, even if they could get one to come out in less than a year. Second, they knew each other and so could keep checking on each other for mistakes which might be fatal, taking care of each other easily and without vanity. Third, they had spent enough time on the sea to have gotten used to danger; after all, handling dynamite is no more dangerous than throwing overboard a heavy anchor whose chain can foul an ankle and drag you after it—you just have to be careful. Fourth, they could take their own time. As a matter of fact, they would have insisted on working at their own pace even if the front office hadn't been right down in the hole with them in the form of President Tully. Their classic Maine cool allowed them to learn the dangerous, unfamiliar job slowly and to pause ever so slightly before acting.

Even so, on one hole they blew when I was around, they left the pump near the hole in the blast area by mistake. As the dust settled, and the geyser from the water in the hole drifted away in mist, we found it lying on its side, having been blown ten feet in the air. I would have yelled something like "Oh my God, the pump!" or "Who the hell left the pump here?" or something. Instead, someone said something like "Well—looks like we forgot the pump," and someone else said, "Guess we did." Pat took off the housing and diagnosed a couple of teeth missing, bent the housing back into shape and looked for the screw which he had dropped getting the housing off ("Can't seem to hang on to that screw"). The pump started but didn't work well, and they knocked off work for the day, Pat saying that he'd go to a nearby city on the mainland and rent another, that he hadn't liked that one (which was his own) much and anyway he could get a couple of coils of cable which they needed. This is the pace to have when you're handling dynamite. It reminds me of the story of one of the mailboat captains years ago, who ran his boat aground on the bar in the Thoroughfare, jumped over the side and walked up to his house for a couple of gallons of paint, saying it was about time he painted the bottom anyway.

By the end of winter all of the holes had been blasted and the poles delivered and laid alongside the road, ready to be raised into position. The piece of heavy equipment needed for this job costs twenty-four thousand dollars, which the power company didn't have, so Pat adapted an available machine to the job. This sounds pretty straightforward until you realize that the equipment to be adapted, called a cherrypicker, consisted of a special truck with two fifteen-foot lengths of steel on top, one joined to the other like an arm and with about the same movements as an arm, on the end of which is a kind of basket in which a man can stand. They are used to repair transformers at the tops of telephone poles, and I suppose they can even be used to pick cherries if you want to make a big production out of picking cherries. The adaptation of this to a pole setter,

according to the Island way of doing things, required that Pat design and manu-
facture—himself—an extension about twenty feet long, capable of lifting a
fifty-foot pole over a foot in diameter to an erect position above the ground,
dropping it into the hole and wiggling it about until straight, the extension
being controlled from up in the air by a set of controls located in the basket.
At one point in the design and construction of this beautiful bastard, it was
discovered that more counterweight to the pole-setting arm was needed, so the
trunk of a large spruce was added, like a great tail, at a carefully determined
angle onto the rear end. The lichen stayed on the freshly cut tree trunk,
and it was a multimaterial marvel.

I don't know what Pat's classmates from his architecture school are
doing, but I doubt if many of them have produced anything as resplendent in
Form and Function as the pole setter, much less built it themselves single-
handed. At one point in their training, architects learn a certain amount of
mechanical engineering; some use it one place, some use it another.

I found that all this innovation had an effect on me. The air conditioner in my
darkroom in New York is awkwardly situated way up near the ceiling, and so I
have to stand on a stepladder every time I want to adjust it. After I had returned
from one trip to the Island, I encountered this problem and in five minutes had
rigged up a device made out of a mop handle with a clamp on the end that held
a wooden stick which allowed me to probe for the adjustment keys. It was on a
smaller scale than the cherrypicker–polesetter, but I wouldn't have been able to
do this before the experience of the Island; I would have been humble before
all that streamlined plastic and would have assumed that, if General Electric
had wanted me to put the air conditioner up near the ceiling, it would have
given me six-foot arms.

We have gotten used to the ability of heavy construction equipment to move
enormous bulk and weight. There is something wonderful about the way a
backhoe, just as the cherrypicker, is based on the design and movement of the
human body, being merely a gigantic steel child scooping out the moat around
its sand castle. The machines are huge and beautiful and effective, but not many
of them get to the Island. Nonetheless, thirty-foot boats and two-ton floats
are hauled up the steep beaches every fall and returned to the water every
spring with equipment no more complicated than a winch on the front of
a truck, cable, pine trunks and rocks. Again, I think it is their familiarity with
the superhuman power of the sea that allows the islanders to have what

seems to me the enormous audacity to attempt such feats. Twice every day a good part of the Atlantic Ocean rises anywhere from seven to ten feet vertically and the power of its movement can perform a number of useful tasks. For instance, if you have to move a one-ton mooring you just haul the chain in taut to your boat at low tide, leaving no slack as you tie one link of the chain to the bow with a short length of line, and then let the rising tide lift the boat and the mooring off the bottom; the load in water weighs less than it does out of the water and can be easily moved to its new location, the rope holding the chain out and the mooring dropped. This is pretty impressive harnessing of a natural force; the tide was probably being used this way before the invention of the wheel. There is also pretty impressive danger attached to it: if you happen to catch any part of yourself in the mooring chain as you cut it free from the buoy, you will be carried over, not to reappear for twelve hours, which is too long to hold your breath, and so you learn early to keep all of the chain over the side during the operation.

There are a number of jobs which require the personal efforts or the personally owned machinery of individuals to accomplish a common purpose (or simply to help each other out) and therefore can be called communal, whether or not the individuals are paid by the town. The job needs doing, the word goes out and people quietly show up at the right time and place. There is no discernible boss, because everybody knows the basic technique so well that any variations made necessary by special problems are figured out on the spot. Nobody is bucking for promotion, so there's no competition to get in the way of an easy efficiency.

In January it became evident that the contractor who was scheduled to haul the town float out of the water, in order to preserve it from any serious ice which might form in the Thoroughfare and for any repairs which it might need, wasn't going to be able to do the job, and so the town, in the person of the first selectman, hired the citizenry to do it.

The final resting place of the float was to be a spot up against a bank about fifty yards above high water in one corner of the town parking lot, which meant that the ton of it had to be hauled straight up the sloping shingle beach onto the paving and then hauled off to one side. The motive power for the straight haul was the winch on the front of Irville Barter's truck, parked and braced up the hill. Because there was no available winch to draw it to one side and no way to anchor it while Irville changed the position of his car, an old road grader,

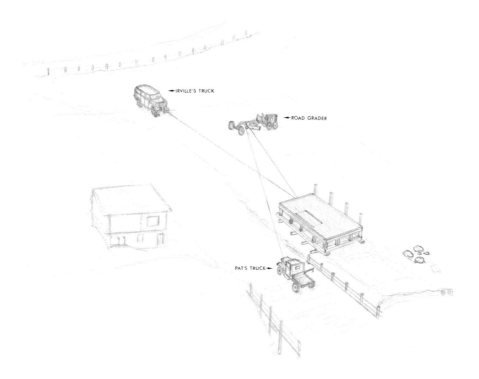

which happened to be around, was parked at the end of *this* projected path, a
pulley secured to it and a second cable from the float run through the pulley
and back to Pat Tully's truck, which was parked at the beginning of the dock.
When the float had been drawn far enough up the beach and onto the land by
Irville's winch, Pat would start up his winch and haul the float on an angle to
its final position via the block on the road grader.

The float was moved over the shingle beach, as well as the hardtop and dirt
of the parking lot, on pine-trunk rollers. The front of the float was raised at
the outset by means of pine-trunk levers and boulder fulcrums and a roller
pushed underneath; as the float moved over this roller, moving it toward the
rear, other pine trunks were put under the front, removed when they came out
from under the back of the float and taken back to the front. Here, directly
demonstrated, were the same methods and the same basic tools which had been
used to build the pyramids: the inclined plane, the pulley, the lever, the wheel.
I don't think I've ever seen them used so directly all at once; I thought that the

kids should be let out of school to watch and be instructed, but it would have been embarrassing ("That's not an applied force, that's Daddy!").

The job is essentially the same as it was seventy years ago, when oxen were used instead of motors. There is the same straining to the limit, but now the strain is more abstractly evidenced in the whine of laboring gears, the ominous creaking of wire cables and the lurches of the road grader, which threatened to capsize until the block was placed lower on it. In the old days, the muscle and bulk of the oxen could have been seen and the shouts of the teamsters heard; the men would have crowded against the flanks of the oxen, pushing, yelling and beating in a noisy, direct effort, as they still do in contests in the country fairs in Maine, where teams of draft horses compete to draw the heaviest loads in the shortest times. Now, when the cable has been attached and the pull is about to start, everyone draws back from the enormous and still somewhat mysterious force which can part a wire cable and send it screaming through the air but which is ominously silent until it does just that. I guess you could get hurt by the oxen too, but they are made of essentially the same stuff as we are, and anyway it was necessary to get close in order to drive them.

When I showed up with my camera to record the event, there were the usual groans, and Pat Tully said, "We don't know what we're doing"; but it was perfectly clear that they knew the job so well that all they had to do was remind each other of the familiar steps and warn each other of the familiar dangers in a kind of shorthand language.

In early May Maurice Barter put his boat in the water. This involved a process somewhat the reverse of the float hauling I've just described, and a number of people were needed. There was no pay involved in this, being a job common to every fisherman and therefore contributed to by most of the men who happened to be around that day. Bill and Wayne Barter, Maurice's fisherman nephews, showed up, as did a few laymen—Pat Haynes (the schoolteacher), Bill Stevens and I.

Maurice's *Sea Pigeon* had lain in its cradle next to Bill's *Payson Kimberly* all winter on the shore of Barter Creek, a tidal inlet named after Robert Barter (Maurice's great-great-great-great-grandfather, I'd guess), who owned eighty-five acres of the land around the head of the creek in 1803. Boats are drawn up in the winter, of course, as there almost always is enough ice in the harbors to damage them, and in any case they are newly painted every year. Typically, the Island fishermen do this themselves, as they tend to do a better and cheaper job than the boatyards. Maurice had done most of the spring work on the boat, and now it was ready to be moved in its cradle from this winter berth well above the high-tide mark to just above where the sea trickles in at low water, so that the wooden planks of the hull could start to swell tight from the salt water of every tide. The *Sea Pigeon* was old and leaky and had to be pampered a bit more than other boats, which can just be launched with the knowledge that they will take in a fair amount of water at first, but not enough to sink, until the hull swells closed. (Few Maine lobster boats have fiberglass hulls, because the wooden hulls last, when cared for, and there are still a lot around. Maurice replaced the *Sea Pigeon* with a second-hand wooden boat at the end of the summer.)

The process of moving the *Sea Pigeon* and her cradle down the beach involved tying a line to a nearby tree and leading it through a block on the front of the cradle, to act as a brake while the cradle was pushed down the incline. The cradle was urged into movement by a lever pushed against the front, and it rode over the first pine-trunk roller placed at its back, all the time braked by the forward line, which could be made fast in an instant by throwing another hitch over the log at the front of the cradle. The rollers rode forward and out from beneath the bow as the *Sea Pigeon* moved stern first down the beach and were carried around to the stern to be placed again in the path of the moving cradle. From all the frivolity while this was going on, you'd never have thought that one false move would send the gigantic rig careening down the beach, to the possible destruction of it and/or one of us.

Again, as with the float hauling, the scale of us and our ropes and tree trunks to what we were moving made us seem like ants, except that ants don't keep breaking themselves up when they're struggling with a particularly large bread-crumb—at least I don't think they do. Maurice wasn't particularly respectful of his boat, and this gave rise to a kind of repartee of gentle insult, which I won't ruin by trying to duplicate because it depends on a deadpan dryness and intricacy which would do any stand-up comic proud. It was a constant stream of banter, in which there was no repetition, in which each exchange led sparely and gracefully to the next.

I think that there is something about the natural difficulties of living on an island that must attract technical virtuosity. Outside expertise and spare parts are not immediately available, and alternate solutions to technical problems must be found all the time. This must lead to a closer examination of machinery which on the mainland is taken for granted. If you can't get a replacement for a complicated automobile engine part from the dealer down the road, you are led into taking it apart and examining how you might fix it. In so doing, you might find out that it is designed to fall apart automatically after a certain period of time, being made of cardboard held together by chewing gum, and certain to emit all sorts of horrible nasty things into the environment. In the quiet of the long winter evenings in your island home, according to this fantasy I have, separated from the noise of the marketplace telling you to get on with it and not buck the system, which knows what everyone wants, you might get angry for long enough to invent, say, the Wankel engine. I know that I was exposed to more *basic* consideration of the environment—disposal of awkward material, full use of natural energy, conservation of natural resources —that winter on the Island than I was in four years of getting literature from environmental organizations, because the Island's environment was small and contained and we had to care for it because it was surrounded by water. This set of necessities had brought together a bunch of amateur mad scientists who were constantly tinkering with things like hull design, learning chess, designing large new machines, putting together iceboats, taking cars apart and the like.

The latest letter from the Island brought the news that Jack and Belvia and Nita and Danny MacDonald have moved into their new house and have sold their old house to a young man and his weaver wife and their children. The young man makes toys out of real materials, like wood. The MacDonalds could have sold their house to summer people for a lot more money, but summer people don't stay on the Island in the winter, sending their kids to the school and producing things which can be held in the hands or looked at or made to run before they are sent away to produce money.

The lumber for the addition to the Skolnikoffs' house in Rich's Cove was brought over from the mainland by helicopter at a saving of time and, therefore, money. I'd heard about this, but I was properly horrified when we came back to the cove from the lovely quiet of the nearby nesting island one morning and heard the noise of it approaching over the treetops. Unfairly, I associate helicopters close up with our invasion of Vietnam and other obscenities, and anyway I hadn't heard anything that loud since the last time I had stood behind a New York City bus, so I yelled at it and highmindedly refused to take its picture until it returned for its tenth trip and couldn't be avoided any longer. Practically everyone on the Island had gathered to see the operation, and I felt angry at

them for admiring this monster of the future, which might cancel out the miles
of open water between paradise and the Main, destroying the Island's islandness.
On further thought, though, I realized that the helicopter lift was just another
example of the Island's audacity, another technical innovation. It fitted into the
long line of solutions to the logistical problems raised by living here.

Know where the first really effective solar generator is going to be developed?

4

ISLAND BASICS

CARS

A lot of the Island's technical ingenuity goes into the maintenance of its cars.
A friend of mine visited the Island several years ago and asked the man who
was then running the mailboat where he might rent one. It was early in the
summer, and the informal taxi service hadn't started, so the mailboat captain
told the visitor to use his, parked near the wharf. He explained that it didn't
have a key but could be started by holding the bare ends of the ignition wire
together and stepping on the accelerator. This easy familiarity and direct
connection with the workings of the automobile engine seemed to impress my
friend as much as the sight of the Cliffs, to which he drove. I think I know why:
the Cliffs road would be a challenge to a Land Rover, and, after traveling the
two miles of it in a car which you'd had to start by holding two wires together,
to arrive at the kind of awe-inspiring place which it is might be like suddenly
finding yourself in the Arctic in your topcoat; the scale of the place suggests
the goal of an elaborately planned expedition, requiring special vehicles, native
guides, pack mules, radio contact with base camp—and all he had done was get
on a boat and borrow somebody's car. Returning, it must have seemed like a
dream.

   Actually, the fewer the intervening gadgets between the driver and the works
of a car—the closer he is to the actual machinery—the more likely he is to get
back from a place like the Cliffs in such a car. It's easier to fix an old engine, in

which the organs are properly exposed and easy to get at, than one of the later models where everything is shrouded in mysterious superfluity—superfluity at least as far as the needs of a car on the Island are concerned. After a few years of Island life, a car tends to be reduced to essentials anyway; these essentials are maintained by Harold van Doren, who, among other things, is the resident mechanic.

I'm not one myself, so I can't make a professional evaluation, but I'd guess that Harold is a complete mechanic. He once told me that he likes the smell of gasoline; having spent a good deal of my childhood getting out of cars to throw up, I find this almost creepy. Aside from this sensual attraction to cars, he is a compulsive fixer, or—more specifically—faced with a piece of machinery which doesn't work, he is not really happy until he has found out what's wrong with it. He may not be able to fix it immediately, lacking a part or a tool, but he has to make the diagnosis. Late one night in April, he and his wife, Olive, Pat and Annie Haynes, the teachers, and I were sitting around at our place, when I mentioned casually that the toilet was stopped up, and that I'd been unable to fix it by the usual methods. Within two minutes he was out in the moonlight trying to open up the pipe to the septic tank. He may like the smell of gasoline, but an open sewer is something else, and I think he was just as happy that I didn't have a wrench large enough to carry out his compulsion to get to the bottom of the problem, but he had to give it a good try. The compulsion didn't require him to come back the next day, because by then he had something else to repair.

What he had to repair was generally scattered around outside the trailer in which he and Olive and their little girl, Amy Dawn, lived. Sometimes engine parts found their way into the trailer, and Olive told me that there was once a disassembled motor all over the living-room floor for three weeks until, fussy woman that she is, she picked it up and put it in a box.

Besides being a complete mechanic, Harold is a complete *Island* mechanic. About twelve years ago Gene Skolnikoff acquired a '37 Pontiac which developed the need for a new condenser. He and Harold went to the car dump, which flowed gently into the sea at Head Harbor, and, at low water, got one out of a car engine which was covered and uncovered with the tide. This same intertidal condenser is successfully condensing away in Gene's car to this day.

Like Pat Tully, Harold is in his thirties and the son of a summer family. He was brought up in Princeton, New Jersey, where his father was a chemist, and the succession of childhood summers caused too strong a hold for him to stay away. After working as a draftsman in a regional planning office on the mainland, he married Olive, who comes from inland Maine, and moved into winter quarters in the trailer, which was parked that winter in town, a hundred yards from the main road up a dirt trail, which came to be known as "the glacier" because it served as a runoff for a little stream nearby and was consequently covered with a thick sheet of ice. The summer of that first year I was on the Island they moved the trailer over to the forty acres on the east side which Harold inherited from his father, on which there is a little log cabin built for them in 1928 by Leon Small. It's this land which is home to Harold and on which he will someday build a proper house. It, the trailer, his garage business (meaning a talent and a toolbox, not a building), hauling and scalloping with Jack MacDonald and, that summer, working for the Point maintenance crew constituted the economic toehold he had on the Island. With all of these he worked normally hard in the winter and abnormally long hours in the summer; some nights he was working on cars by battery-powered floodlight until midnight and getting up at 5 A.M. for his regular job at the Point. Olive worked in the store that winter and cleaned cottages in the summer to help out. I'd guess that on the mainland, working as a draftsman or as a mechanic, he'd have a much easier time of it and now would be comfortably rising within the framework of an organization. But he wouldn't be on the Island. It's obviously hard for Olive, just as it is for the other young wives, to live in the constricted social life of the Island (in number of people at least), and there is the worry about Amy Dawn's being removed from immediate medical care and not having as many children to play with as she would on the mainland. You could say that Harold has a kind of pioneer challenge to enrich his life, which Olive can't feel as directly, these being times when women don't have the opportunity of working at the sides of their husbands, clearing the land, tilling the soil and fighting off the Indians. It's harder for her, but I think that the quality of their lives on the Island tips the balance.

After a few years of taking care of the Island's cars, Harold has acquired a little fleet of automotive invalids, and our first car, a '62 Rambler, was one of these. There's something absolutely ridiculous about driving on the dirt roads of the Island in a car which has the pretensions of grandeur found in most recent cars. They're slung too low for the vagaries of the roads' surfaces, and the front seat envelops you in a kind of armchair, placing your line of vision two inches above the dashboard and making it impossible to see anything closer than ten feet from the front of the car—a distance which on the Island's roads can include two ditches, a bog, the edge of a cliff and a ten-point buck. The Rambler was one of these, but it moved and was capable of being stopped, so we set off happily. We returned in a few minutes, asphyxiated, as it had the kind of exhaust leak which literally requires you to drive with your head out the window. Until it rained too hard this would have been O.K., if the window hadn't been so high that you couldn't get your head out of it anyway.

Our second car from Harold was a '63 Impala, which had a magic transmission: the shift handle on the steering column was connected to a gear box in which there was the usual assortment of gears, but floating around in such a haphazard juxtaposition that it would take me anywhere from thirty seconds to five minutes to find first; for the first three days I managed to go from first to second about thirty-five percent of the time before giving up and either returning to first or waiting until we reached the top of a rise and I could get up enough speed to go into high. My percentage of success in this maneuver rose about twenty points in the next three days but never got beyond fifty-five percent. Continuing from second, I could get it into high about eighty-five percent of the time. I got it into reverse maybe three times in all. In order to shift, you had to put it into neutral and probe for the next gear, the search ending in the limp failure of another version of neutral or in the exhilarating sensation of meshing gear teeth. There was no door to the trunk, and the body there hadn't rusted away enough to provide drainage, so the car had to be bailed out after every rainstorm. This was appropriate to the surroundings.

I actually *bought* the third car I drove—a '66 Chevy—and it was brought to the Island on Russ Deveraux's barge. About the third day I had it, I bent the tie rod on the Cliffs road and then cracked the cylinder head by pouring cold water into the radiator too soon after the car had overheated as the result of a leak which had developed in the cooling system. I began to acquire the reputation of a car killer, but actually I was just relearning the automotive basics which I had known when I was driving an ambulance in the war but which I'd forgotten in the pampered years since. Harold removed the cylinder head for diagnosis and left the car outside the house, and I renewed my struggles with the mystery-transmission Impala.

The next morning I was due to go hauling with Phil Alley at 5 A.M.; I staggered out of the house at 4:45 and into the first car which presented itself, which happened to be the cylinder-headless Chevy. I cranked the starter motor a few times without result and then got out and angrily raised the hood. I generally do this when a car won't start; on account of my deep mechanical savvy, I can pretty much tell whether the motor's there or not, and anyway, if I raise the hood with enough authority, the car may be bluffed into thinking

I'm master and start up. This time I raised the hood and found the engine in flames—not just smoke, but a real bonfire crackling away—started, as any half-awake fool could tell, by all that gasoline which my furious pumping of the accelerator had scattered about. On my way to get the fire extinguisher all I could think of was the Island burning up by my hand. I'd always wanted to see what would come out of a fire extinguisher if you pressed the button, and there it was—all that nice white foam, which really did put out the burning gasoline.

I didn't like that car much anyway; the next one was a four-wheel-drive International Scout, capable of climbing the highest mountains and fording the deepest rivers. For starters its water pump gave out, and I was restrained by my conscience and a few strong men from swiping one from the Scout of a summer resident who had been particularly kind to me on my first trip to the Island. Pat Haynes put in the replacement I got from the Main, and I thereby learned where the water pump was and what it looked like. A couple of days later in the middle of a cold spell the gas line developed a leak. I found Harold over at Jack MacDonald's, where he was helping to repair Jack's lobster traps. He stopped off by and by, got a coil of copper tubing from the back of his truck and, lying on his back in the five-degree cold, sculpted a new gas line. Later that day, on my way to Moore's Harbor, the gas tank fell off. I was going along, nice as you please, when there was this horrible crash. I got out of the car, which is another of my strong moves, and there it was—a real, honest-to-goodness gas tank, hanging by the one bright entrail which Harold had installed that morning. I'd never seen one before and it was very educational. I went back to the MacDonalds', where Harold, work for the day having finished, was playing Go with Pat Haynes and Jack, while Belvia and the kids watched TV. I expected to be told to forget the new car for God knows how long until a new gas tank could be imported. Instead, they came down the road to the Scout, disconnected the tank, joined another piece of copper tubing to the new gas line and ran it up through a hole someone knocked in the floor to a five-gallon can placed inside the car. There were at that time three other cars which had this same artificial digestive tract, and it worked fine, particularly as I had given up smoking a couple of years before and so I didn't blow up. After a couple of months I got a new gas tank and it could be said that the Scout had had all the bugs removed—dramatically but effectively—and that it had started on its long life as an Island car, stripped down but reliable.

Miss Lizzie, when she was a young woman

(l. to r.) Lizzie, Llewellyn and Ava Rich among their classmates at the east side school

Where the mail gets delivered after its travels through rain, snow, heat of day
or gloom of night (not to mention in this case fog, winter vapor and high
seas) is the Island post office, a small building which served as John Turner's
confectionery before it was moved from its original location up the mountain
above town on the road to Head Harbor. Its hours are the most lenient in the
entire postal service, as it is also the home of the postmistress, Elizabeth Rich,
formally referred to by the winter and summer residents as Miss Lizzie, by the
winter residents who are near her age as Lizzie and by most of the year-round
kids as Aunt Lizzie. I suppose if you were really mad at her you could call her
Miss Rich.

Miss Lizzie was born in 1893 in Rich's Cove, in a house near the one we
rented during the summer, and she went to the school in town ("What little
I learned, I learned there") with her brother Llewellyn and sister Ava.
Llewellyn died in 1960 and Ava, who was very close to her, died in the old
family house in 1970. The pictures of the three of them suggest that they had a
pretty happy childhood, which Miss Lizzie wouldn't deny although what she
seems to remember now is the work. She walked to school, a distance of about
two miles, and after school she remembers homework, and a great many chores
—like knitting the bait bags which are still used in lobster traps. At the age of
thirteen she started to work as a housekeeper—first for a dollar a week for a
summer visitor who lived down the east side about three miles away and then,
at the age of sixteen, for John Turner, a resident. In 1926 she became postmistress, and in 1963 she retired at the mandatory age of seventy. The day
after she retired, the post office was converted to the status of rural station
and she resumed her duties without change under the title of Clerk in Charge.

Miss Lizzie has reached the age, after living on the Island all her life,
where people begin to think of her as a beloved institution, and although
this has certain advantages for her, I think she fights the characterization. She
has also reached the age where people like me have the nerve to try to describe
her qualities, to tell fond stories about her. I find that this is hard, because
every story seems to have its contradiction in another quality which rises to the
surface and then submerges—such as sudden flashes of great wit breaking
through a general manner of dry disapproval. Also, as much as I am deeply
fond of her, I am in awe of her, as I was in awe of my grandmother, who was
a *grande dame* capable of arousing great fear by her disapproval and, therefore,

great happiness by her approval, or even relief by the mere withholding of her disapproval.

I've heard it said that many of the people on the Island also have a good deal of awe mixed in with their love of her. She has a withering dryness, she seems to be unaffected by anything, and she says "hmph!" a good deal. She and her sister, Miss Ava, were pillars of the church, as she still is, and the story told is that the two of them would position themselves in such a way as to check the attendance, so that if you hadn't been there the previous Sunday you would be reminded of it, not directly by anything either of them would say but simply by the force of their presence. I have found myself about to use language in this book which is a general part of my vocabulary but which I've not used out of respect for (fear of?) Miss Lizzie. Why does she have this power? It's not only age, or a lifetime of living in one place, or that she can be "difficult," because if this was the case all strong old women would rule matriarchies, and only some of them do. It isn't only that the Island, being a true community, respects its old members and values them as a repository of experiences. Rather, more than anything, I think Miss Lizzie has earned her power. At her age she is still recognizable as the little girl to the left of Llewellyn.

When she broke her hip three years ago, she became dependent on her neighbors to an extent that would be acceptable to many other women of her age and community position but which I expect was painful to her. She has a car which she cannot drive any more and so must depend on Maurice, who is her nephew, to drive her around. When the ground is free of snow, she gets herself to the well outside of her house with the assistance of her walker, which she has to use always, lets down a pail, draws the water up and lashes the pail to the top rail of the walker. By her own admission, she may only have half a pail when she gets back, which I can understand if I imagine myself performing the same task. In the winter, when there's snow on the ground, she appoints one person to get her water, and if that person can't do it she will go a long time before she will let anyone else substitute. Someone regularly brings her groceries, and one of the kids mows her lawn in the summer.

For many things she is dependent on her last-remaining relatives on the Island, Maurice and Helen Barter, and her neighbors, but she is dreadfully impatient with having to depend on anyone even to this degree. She insists on picking up the floor sweepings in a dustpan, hanging laboriously on the walker, even when someone else is in the room and offers to help. Every last bit of self-

sufficiency is jealously held on to, and every acceptance of help is a battle lost.
It's like when Julie fell down some subway steps a few years ago, she found
herself snapping angrily to the people who came to help her that she was
perfectly all right, as the result of public mortification.

Miss Lizzie resents age and resists it by working as hard as she can in the
same way that many women resist it by getting all done up. I've helped her up
steps and into cars a few times, and I've noticed that the trick is to help her
not one whit more than is absolutely necessary; it's best to support the walker,
not her, and not to expect any expressions of gratitude. What's amazing is her
agility with the walker; trying to help her, I realized that she had gotten the
knack of how to use it most efficiently, and that, if one caught on too, one could
be a help but, if not, one could send her flying. This is an agility born of
impatience with her condition, the old habit of taking care of herself and a
lifetime of climbing in and out of boats and up and down rocks. Liz Cousins
drove her to the nearest city a couple of times the winter before last to do some
shopping. She offered to go around with her and help her to cross streets, but
Miss Lizzie treated the jump from the Island to the middle of a city with
contempt and, while Liz held her breath, pushed off across the busiest of the
city's intersections. She made it to the other side perfectly all right.

This defiance is accomplished with a fair amount of the dry humor that is
evident in the little girl of the school picture. She hardly gets out of the house at
all, and one day in leaving I said, "See you later"; she replied, "I expect I'll
be here." Jim Wilson ordered a new exhaust system from the Main, which had
arrived and been left for him at the post office. He'd collected his mail, been told
about it and had walked out without it; as Miss Lizzie later looked at the ten
feet of futuristically curved, mummy-wrapped tubing standing against the wall
in the little vestibule she remarked that if it had been a little bit bigger he
might have noticed it.

Julie and I once visited her right after she had washed her hair, which was
in ringlets from the curlers she had just taken off and which she hadn't combed
out. Miss Lizzie doesn't often volunteer explanations because her habits and
appearance are so carefully controlled that they're rarely necessary, but she
had to explain then, "otherwise you'd think I'd gone crazy." She went on to
explain that Ava had always wanted to cut her hair, but that she'd always
resisted, because "I know the way I look now—wouldn't know the way I'd look
then." That statement has the kind of simple strength that could bring down
the entire international fashion industry if it were spread about.

Miss Lizzie doesn't square dance any more, but there are those who remember the strength of her swing in the Lady of the Lake, and she is a lady of small stature. The memory is recent—from the summer before she had her accident.

She doesn't treat the condition of spinsterhood with a great deal of gravity; she once explained to me her concern about whoever is running the mailboat on stormy days by saying that she has no man of her own to worry about, so she has to worry about everyone else's.

Thunderstorms seem to be the only fear Miss Lizzie expressed to me. She won't put her hair up in curlers in the middle of one, and she smiles when she says this, knowing it's a fear not commonly held. I don't know though— maybe she's right; a friend of ours who was a distinguished physicist used to go out and sit in his car during a thunderstorm, as the tires isolated him from the ground and therefore gave him complete protection.

People noticed that Miss Lizzie didn't show up at a number of town events the first year I was on—mainly town meeting—and they were worried that this was a kind of withdrawal. Perhaps it was. On the other hand the post office is an island information center which is open during the waking hours of her day, and so there is usually someone sitting around there, and in the summer there is great activity. Even in the middle of the winter I don't imagine she gets terribly lonely. Most of the summer people correspond with her regularly, and the letters she sends them, to judge by the ones I've gotten, are diligently comprehensive; they consist of factual reportings of who's on- and who's off-island and why (like the column she writes for the "Salt Air Society" section of the Main's newspaper) and news of the lives of the other summer residents she has heard from. She serves as an instrument of communication—a noble calling. On her first trip to New York a few years ago, she was sitting on the train probably feeling surrounded by strangers, when whom should she see but an old summer friend from the Island. After all these years of maintaining connections between friends it was nice that there was this chance reciprocation.

The most evident quality of Miss Lizzie's house is its smallness. The post office consists of one corner of the front room, partitioned off behind a wall of standard glass-fronted boxes, interrupted by the usual post office window. The room and most of the house is heated by a kerosene stove in the corridor leading back to the tiny kitchen and bedroom. The counter from the building's former existence as John Turner's confectionery almost fills the room and generally holds a pile of trail maps, post cards of the Island and copies of the Main newspaper for sale, and an open notebook in which anyone can record items for the paper's column of news from the various islands. Above it hangs a cage with a parakeet, and all around are the loving accumulations of years (a lobster claw of record proportions, a row of plastic deer, various works of art by summer people, and the like). There are three chairs for Miss Lizzie and her pretty constant visitors.

Toward the spring of the first year I was on, it became evident that the post office was going to fall down around Miss Lizzie's ears unless there were major repairs. She was set in her opinion that all that was needed was to repair the sills, whereas the men of the Island whom she consulted—mainly Maurice —knew that, once the poor old building was opened up, it would be found that there wasn't a solid enough piece of the structure to nail a sill onto, and that it would be cheaper to build a new house than repair the old. It was one of those situations which seem to be common on the Island: there was a major job which needed doing, everybody acknowledged the need and there was a capability to take care of the need, but first a complicated set of emotional and social needs had to be met. They were indeed met and by the first snowfall the kitchen and bedroom at the rear of the post office–parlor had been torn down and replaced.

SCHOOL

The Island school goes from kindergarten through the eighth grade—as do most schools on Maine islands. This means that when an Island youngster finishes eighth grade his parents must move off or he must board with mainland friends or relatives while he goes to high school. The first year I was on, the enrollment varied from six pupils in the fall and spring to four in the middle of the winter. The eighth-grader would go to high school off-island in the fall; the seventh, fifth, fourth, third and second grades consisted of one pupil apiece—at the peak of enrollment, that is.

The teaching staff was a young couple, Pat and Ann Haynes. Annie, who grew up and went to school and college in Vermont, was the head teacher, having taught before on the West Coast, and Pat, her assistant, is a mechanical engineer and recent graduate of MIT. That was their first year, and they were there through a chain of circumstances and conditions which, I think, says a great deal about the Island and its future. The job of schoolteacher had become vacant when Ted Hoskins, the summer minister who had stayed on to teach the previous winter, returned to a mainland parish. Pat and Annie, who had traveled around Europe a little bit after Pat's graduation and who were not totally enthusiastic about settling into the kind of life which was indicated by an engineering degree, came to the Island as campers early that summer. They had the usual reaction to the place, heard that the job was open, applied to the Island school board and were accepted. I'm sure that the alternatives open to Pat weren't so unattractive to him as to have caused a headlong flight, and both of them are serious people, so their application wasn't made on the basis of naïve romanticism; they wouldn't have gotten the job if it had been. It's just that there are a lot of very talented and energetic young adults in this country who are unwilling to be tucked into the corporate structure and that the Island is pretty seductive. The results are mutually advantageous: the school has good teachers, and two more people have come face to face with a community and have benefited from the encounter.

Given the fact that daily transportation of the children by boat to a mainland school would be the ultimate inconvenience of living on the Island and that people would feel foolish staying on under such conditions, it becomes clear that the existence of the Island is based on the existence of the school; this follows a direct equation. There is no minimum limit to the number of pupils necessary to keep the school open, but if the last pupil should leave and the school be closed, it would become very hard to get the regional authorities to reopen it for any newcomers. Thus the Island, having lost its young families, would not attract other young couples who have or expect children. As the remaining old people got older they would have no way to get off the Island, since there would be no young men to carry them onto a boat when they got sick, and the Island would become uninhabited during the winter. I can think of only a very few of the present summer residents who would want to come to the Island if they and a few nonresident caretakers were the only ones on it. The land might be used for a number of things, but the Island would cease to exist.

This basic dependence on the existence of the school and the need for young immigrants is fairly common on the Maine islands. The situation is sometimes handled ingeniously. The people of one of the islands off the coast, faced a few years ago with the departure of their own schoolchildren, adopted a number of foundlings and thereby kept their school open.

Of course, the school could keep flunking one of the eighth-graders year after year until relief arrived.

It may be the result of my deep bias, but it seems to me that there is more concern for education on the Maine coast than in other parts of the country. The very precision and rhythm of the language suggest a deep exposure to education and the written word; the slips from correct usage—such as "they was"—are more part of a patois than the result of sloppiness. The reticence which I've talked about earlier as modesty could also be, in part, an unwillingness to speak until the thought can be expressed precisely. It seems that there is a standard of verbal clarity; people may not read a great deal now, but their parents did and this affects their lives.

At the risk of being provincial, I would say that this *environment* of education is part of the cultural heritage of New England, but more specifically it may come from the exposure to other cultures which is the inevitable result of sea trade, and by this standard, the Maine coast has been in the middle of things for 150 years. These days, education has a very immediate function, in that it is impossible to travel on the water for long without using math, even in the most offhand methods of navigation. The expectation of having to coax a recalcitrant marine engine into life far away from the nearest professional mechanic many times might easily give a student an extra sense of the value of physics, as being surrounded by the mechanical beauty of fishing gear might also.

Whatever the general reasons, schools seem to have been built and staffed at the drop of a hat on the Island a hundred years or so ago. Around the turn of the century a family named Gross settled in Head Harbor, and so the town built a special school for the education of their children, which closed when they moved back to the mainland after a few years. There was a school on the east side which at one point had a larger enrollment than the school in town, although it had closed by the time of Miss Lizzie's education. Marjorie Smith, who died during my first summer on, was Dean of Women at Syracuse University, and had spent her second-grade year in this school; she had been sick, and her parents thought that the Island, where they lived in the summer, would be healthier for her than her city home. Her connection with the Island was other than that of a summer resident (she was a direct descendant of the Kimballs, who settled Kimball's Island, and related to Ben Smith, who ran a boardinghouse there in the eighties; she was also related to the Turners), so it was a fairly natural thing for her parents to have decided. She was taught by Miriam Turner, of the Island, and her schoolmates were Miss Lizzie and Isabel MacDonald. In the 1880s William Turner went from the Island school, which then went through the twelfth grade, straight to MIT and then on to the Purdue faculty and a full professorship; he had a house on the Island which is still known as "the Professor's house," and he continued to think of the Island as his real home.

In 1910 the town paid $3.50 per week for the education of its children

—$3 directly to the teacher and fifty cents to the townsperson who provided the teacher's room and board.

There seemed to be an atmosphere of informal industry about the school every time I dropped in, and what was surprising to me was that my visits were accepted so casually by the teachers and the kids; everybody went on with what they were doing, which was different from my own school experience, when a visitor provided a welcome relief from what was pretty near complete tension. Of course, the condition of three to six students, all in different grades, being taught by two teachers produces an absolutely unique educational experience, in which three-quarters of the time is spent in individual tutoring. This amount of individual attention which each of the kids got was wonderful, but there might be a disadvantage in that none of them had peers in the same grade against whom they could measure themselves, and they learned in a kind of limbo. I felt that Pat's and Annie's jobs weren't made particularly easier by the small number of students, as they were tempted to push the limits of their involvement with each of the kids and their jobs tended to be always with them. I don't know enough to make a judgment or even an analysis of this unique educational situation, but the school seemed like a place where a good deal of learning was taking place with a minimum amount of pressure.

The regional school authorities set a minimum required accomplishment, which is measured by progress in various workbooks for different subjects, but otherwise the schedule is left up to the teachers. For Pat and Annie the school day would start at 7:45, with Lisa being dropped off at their house across from the school by Dotty Dodge in the pickup truck–school bus, while she went to pick up Danny, Nita, Payson and Heidi, who live at the other end of town. Ben lived next door to the school. Lisa would help Pat and Annie eat their breakfast, and when Dotty had delivered the rest of the kids, one of them, whose turn it was, would raise the flag and feed the gerbils. The gerbils, small rodents somewhat like guinea pigs, were used to some educational purpose, I'm sure, but seemed to be more mascots than anything else. Except in the case of bad weather, the entire group would then run around a nearby field, it being considered wise to wear the kids out or get the blood circulating, or something, before the long academic morning.

From 8:30 to 9:30 Pat would take about half of the student body and teach the three of them math and science while Annie would take the other three for reading. Because of the difference in grades, this would involve a series of tutoring sessions. At 9:30 the groups would switch around. At 10:15 there was a fifteen-minute recess, and except when there was too much snow on the ground, everybody including the teachers would play dodge ball. At 10:30 there was a short period of science or social studies, and at 11 everyone watched educational TV. The television period overlapped into lunch, which more or less started at 11:15.

Most of the kids brought their lunches to school, and Pat and Annie would eat at their house across the road, although I remember a couple of nice vegetarian, hundred-percent-organic picnics with them on the school steps in the spring. After lunch there would be an hour of reading aloud by Annie—in good weather, outside on the ground where everyone could make doodles in the dirt. Strangely, nature stories were the most popular in this place of constant exposure to a degree of wildness which most kids in this country are lucky to experience once a year. There would be another academic period from 12:45 to 1:30, afternoon recess from 1:30 to 1:45 and then art (mostly linoleum cutting) and crafts (mostly birdhouses). This would be the time for added attractions, like Bill Stevens, the ranger, giving a talk about animals, or me, a demonstration of photographic printing. At 2:20 everyone cleaned up the schoolhouse, and school was out at 2:30 in time to make it to the store—which was where I first had seen Pat in my first week on the Island, coming in from the downpour outside, bearded and dripping, with a small child under his poncho. I had wondered who he was.

Bennie graduated in the spring, but five-year-old Kimberly Barter and four-year-old Amy Dawn van Doren and Bobby Turner entered the kindergarten, so there is a net gain of two.

STORE

In any small community, rural or urban, the storekeeper performs a public function as much as he operates a business. Food is a permanent and pervasive requirement, so there is an interdependence between the grocery store and its customers which is as close as any business can get to a marriage and still masquerade as a business. Traditionally, when times are bad, it is the store-keeper who is saddled with the responsibility of keeping his neighbors alive by extending credit; it is a responsibility he accepts or he goes out of business, because his fortunes are bound up with the community. I suspect that this is less of a problem in Maine than elsewhere, not because the state is not poor but because State-of-Mainers will go to great lengths to stay out of debt. For example, I've been told that it is fairly common for someone building a house to lay the foundations with the money he can spare, then wait until he can afford to put up the risers and continue like this in steps rather than going to a bank for a loan to build the whole house at once.

On the Island, the store is the community storehouse. People can go to the Main for their groceries and do so on the mailboat or their own boats about half the time, but it would be insupportable not to have a store for those times when they can't. This is not only a question of logistics; people could store emergency supplies, and if the Island was cut off for a long period of time, food could be landed by helicopter, I suppose, but the store is one of those things which stand for the life of the Island; without it the Island would not be a community but just a group of people living in isolation. This is evident in the recent history of local storekeeping: each time the job became open, it was taken almost reluctantly. In the nineteenth century, the store was run by Clyde Turner and stood next to the lobster cannery. There were also smaller stores in Rich's Cove and Head Harbor and on York Island, which sold canned goods, a few staples, kerosene and, later, gas, but no fresh meat. About 1910 John K. Barter kept the town store in a building which retained that function until 1971. When Cecil Barter, his successor, died in the mid-fifties, there was nobody terribly anxious to take over, and so Arthur Tully, a summer resident and Pat Tully's father, bought the store and a succession of residents ran it. I get the impression that none of them particularly wanted the job but knew it had to be done and hoped until the last moment that somebody else would offer to do it before they had to—like a tableful of men in a restaurant trying to outfumble each other into paying the check.

Like most small grocery operations it is a community function rather than a good business. The logistics of getting provisions from a wholesaler on the mainland and transporting them to the Island in enough quantity to prevent a shortage while at the same time avoiding a surplus of perishables is a big enough problem to require a computer. A couple of families buy milk on the Main one week and you have to throw out ten quarts of spoiled milk and take the loss: the next week they stay on the Island and need their milk.

The old store building is now vacant; Pat Tully operates his propane, gasoline and kerosene business from tanks in front and alongside of it, and the building itself serves as an oversized receptacle for the charge slips which people push through the front-door mail slot telling how much gas they've taken from the self-service pump. The new store, built and opened in 1971, is owned and operated by Russ and Jean Deveraux. Russ is an entrepreneur, which makes him something of an enigma in Maine. He tends to like large projects; a couple of years ago, for example, annoyed by a couple of boulders on the bar off Nathan's Island which tended to complicate the passage into the Thoroughfare, he landed a bulldozer on the tiny island and cleared them off.

I've spoken of his invention of the specially raked trailer for the landing of groceries. Along the same lines is the twenty-foot vessel looking something like a tiny tugboat painted bright yellow (and hence called the *Yellow Submarine*) which he uses to tow car barges and carry groceries out to the Island, and the seventy-foot derelict freighter which he bought cheap on the chance that he might want to do something with it. All of this innovation and boldness is loosely rationalized by his marine contracting business. He and Jean live on the mainland, on land which was acquired by his Huguenot ancestors over two hundred years ago, but they had been visiting the Island for years, and the insanity of trying to run the store there must have appealed to him, not to mention all the qualities of the Island itself. They built the store and a house next to it for themselves, and they lived on the Island most of the spring, summer and fall and in their mainland home most of the winter. When they weren't on the Island, the store was tended by Maybel Chapin, Olive van Doren or Belvia MacDonald.

Russ and Jean figure that about half of the groceries bought by the Island are bought in the store and about half on the Main. The stock consists of frozen meat and vegetables, a few fresh vegetables sometimes, dairy products, bread and a fair amount of canned goods. There is a hardware section in the back room which doesn't seem to me to be serious. During the winter I was on, the stock was replenished once a week, with an occasional extra trip for bread and milk, except for periods of shortage, which Olive would handle with joyous salesmanship (*"Sure,* we got it"—pause—"Well, how about—?"). I wasn't bothered much by this, being a bachelor for a lot of the time and therefore living on peanut butter and whiskey. In the spring and summer, when more people came on, the provisioning trips rose to about two a week; Jean would do the shopping by station wagon from suppliers on the mainland and deliver either to the *Yellow Submarine* or the mailboat.

Many Maine stores of this size are on a cash-and-carry basis, which, I gather, just means they don't have any formal billing arrangement. On the Island in winter, people work up a bill and generally pay every week—some after longer periods—a totally informal arrangement based on mutual responsibility and trust. The summer people generally put down a deposit to be drawn against, as a method of supplying the store with working capital.

In the middle of the winter the store was open for three hours in the middle of the day, which is enough time to sell groceries to twenty-seven people. If it was an after-hours emergency, and if Olive wasn't isolated at home by the glacier leading up to the van Doren trailer, she could be picked up and driven to the store to open it, sell, and be driven home. Being a new store and spare architecturally, it didn't invite habitual congregation, as had the old store, which in its day was the community gathering place, I'm told. There was no place except the ice-cream freezer to sit on or even lean against, but tradition is deep, and you could sometimes find Jack MacDonald or Gordon Chapin hanging around in quiet periods between fishing chores, while their respective wives tended store. There's really not space enough for a stove, cracker barrel and chairs, which would probably be scorned as too corny anyway, so maybe the ice-cream freezer will have to do. In the summer, there was a porch outside with benches, and a small luncheonette concession, and the store was open full time six days a week.

I gather that the store is a losing proposition, primarily because Russ and Jean don't live on the Island full time and have to pay a storekeeper what might otherwise make the operation break even or put it slightly in the black. Jean told me they've received offers to sell, but only to those who want to run the store in the summer, when there is a chance of profit; they say they would only sell to someone who would provide year-round service—ideally an islander. Let's see . . . There's electricity and a lot of water so I could put a darkroom in the back . . . Julie and I could learn how to add and subtract . . . how about the *Yellow Submarine?* The only problem is it's too much work.

Downtown, autumn

Downtown, spring

Harold and Elthea Turner

The former store and present gas pump

Rich's Cove at high and low tides

Town Meeting—Noyes MacDonald and Maurice Barter
Town Meeting—a vote

Town Meeting—Isabel MacDonald, Town Clerk, and Belvia MacDonald, Moderator

The launching of the *Sea Pigeon*

Maurice Barter

A derelict near Boom Beach

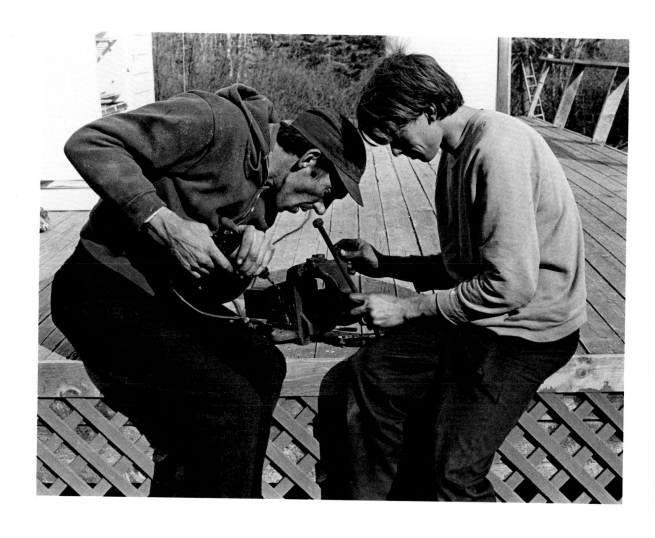

Jack MacDonald and Harold van Doren, working on an engine part

A derelict, deep in the woods

The Skolnikoffs' '37 Pontiac

Dennis Eaton, who died a couple of years before my time on the Island, saved almost everything. Things like the top of a steel drum might come in handy. There was no particular place to discard things, and so they hung around in the grass until they rotted or were used. A friend of his says that he always meant to do something about the stuff lying around but just managed to get it assembled in one spot before he died. Maybe he meant by "doing something about it" that he ought to throw some of it away, or organize it into neater piles or make an inventory or something, but on an island where you have to go to the mainland to get practically anything you need and where people retain the ancient ability to convert past material into present use in pretty ingenious ways, it makes sense to hoard.

The desk came from the old east side school

A boiler. Why, when it was discarded, was it left here? A general answer might be that living on the Island is hard, and so the object bought new in the bright store is particularly welcome—evidence of the vain hope that man *really* dominates this particular environment. Certainly, Maine people do not buy things easily and so do not rid themselves easily of things which are no longer useful. If it was a mistake to buy the thing in the first place, it would be even harder to give up the hope that the mistake hadn't been complete and that the thing might find its true use later on.

This is what's left of a dip net I found on the shore of Rich's Cove. Herring were caught in the cove, as they are still caught in other coves on the coast, by the method of stop-seining, in which the cove is closed off by a net drawn across its opening after the herring have come in. The fish are gathered into a small enclosure, called a purse, and nowadays are sucked from this into the hold of the dealer's boat through what amounts to a large vacuum hose. Thirty years ago, they were dipped from the purse into barrels with the dip net. The herring which came into the cove were also caught by the simpler method of attracting them to the light of burning cotton waste in an iron basket arrangement, called a dragon, secured to the bow of a peapod. As the fish massed around the boat, they would be dipped inside, until the men were standing up to their hips in herring.

It is a reminder of the abundance of the past.

Amy Dawn van Doren

Harold van Doren

Miss Lizzie

School

Pat Haynes with Heidi Heline. Ben MacDonald in rear

Annie Haynes with Danny MacDonald

The schoolhouse, winter and summer

Lisa Turner at the school Halloween party

Boom Beach

The top of the mountain ridge

The birch grove on the mountain ridge

The road through town

A house at Moore's Harbor

Moss at the base of a pine

Scattered over the Island are places where wild orchids grow. These locations are more or less secret, as once the flowers are picked, they're gone forever.

My year of regular visits to the Island began in autumn. This is a special time for people on the Maine coast. The two-month summer is over, and, with it, the bright hectic intrusion of summer visitors. This is the time that most people take vacations, or at least take a long breath before the closing-in of winter. The tourists have gone, and the coast is theirs.

Generally, there is a clarity in the air which is purer than the clearest days of the summer, and, in the mildness of Indian Summer, a softness which I never would have thought possible in these northern parts.

Contrarily, the sea hardens; a fifteen-knot wind pushes up waves which are steeper and higher than the same wind would ever have caused in the summer. I'd heard the autumn air described as "heavier," which I'd thought was a figure of speech until I remembered that cold could actually cause the air to contract and gain added power to push the sea around. We felt this difference when we arrived in our small boat soaked to the skin to take up residence for the first time that fall. I hadn't expected that the passage of three weeks from Labor Day would make that much difference; these waters which I'd known all my life in the summer had changed utterly, and bright days of northwest wind, which in summer constituted a wet challenge, were now ominous in the unfamiliar strength of the waves.

The head of Rich's Cove at low tide

A maple in the middle of a spruce forest

Fernbrake

Autumn blueberry leaves

Ferns near an old stone wall
Blueberry bush

Foam lying in the snow-covered rockweed at Boom Beach

Sometimes there's not even snow
Everything's scarce
My Aunt Lizzie is nice
And I want to know what happens to her
I skate
And that's it.

                              Juanita MacDonald
                        Grade 3 of the Island School

WINTER CONDITIONS

It's not the entire picture of winter on the Island, but Nita's poem covers a fair amount of ground. Living in comfortable circumstances in the city, where cold and snow are sometimes inconvenient but more often prerequisites for good skiing on the weekend, I had lost the specific knowledge of winter—the kind of knowledge which makes you really long for spring, not as a change but as a relief. The Island draws in on itself, and a child might get to wondering about an old friend who had been driven from her consciousness by the activity of the summer.

Out in the bay the average temperature is about five degrees warmer than on the mainland, where it is about ten degrees higher than the interior; the cold is not the dry, intense kind which grips most of New England for three months of the year, but I have seldom felt as much bite as I did the few times I walked around the shore exposed to the northwest wind. In summer the wind from that direction is welcome, as it clears the fog; in winter it brings bitter cold and snow. This is the same northwest wind which froze a carton of milk sitting on the floor *inside* Ted Hoskins' heated and (he thought) insulated house one night during the hard winter the year before I came to the Island.

If it gets cold enough, as it does for some time most winters, the upper section of the bay can freeze over. In 1857, for example, it froze from its head to about twenty-five miles out, isolating the Island as well as a couple of other large islands nearby. By January 25 it was impossible to get to the Island, and the bay stayed that way for eight weeks. In the winter of 1935 Long Island

Sound near New York froze over except for a hundred-yard channel in the middle which was kept open primarily by the passage of the freighters which used it all the time. I was nine years old at the time, and I remember the wonder of carefully walking out over the ice pack; things seemed quite dramatic to me. In Maine at that very same time, early February, 1935, there were four days in which no word was received from the Island. The news account of the isolation doesn't mention it, but I presume that there were no radios in operation then. People on the Main worried, and a National Guard plane flew over and dropped a message asking if everything was O.K. The reply was tied to a rope strung between a rake and a pole held by two men and picked up on a hook by the low-flying plane. It read:

Thank you very much. We have plenty of supplies so far. No one sick. Got our mail yesterday, the first time in over a week. Our mail boat trying to get to [the Main] now. Thank you so much.
                              C. W. Turner

The Maine Seacoast Mission operates a vessel, the *Sunbeam,* which plies the coast on various errands of Christian comfort to the outlying islands. I have the impression that it is called to fewer errands now than its crew would like—what with helicopters, radio transmission, telephones (on some islands) and television being a real, or an apparent, link to the outside world —but in the recent past they had an occasional chance to perform dramatically. A news account from the winter of 1943, during which the Island was icebound for six days, describes the *Sunbeam* as getting as close as possible to the shore, whereupon a group of volunteers from the boat, led by a man with a pick pole to test the ice, carried the mail to a group of Island men who had come out to meet them. The Islanders reported that all was well. ". . . A very brief meeting and we hurried back to the boat for it was snowing hard, and darkness was only an hour away."

This and the other story give the impression that every time there was a snowstorm a whole bunch of eager Samaritans rushed out, expecting the worst, only to find that the situation was under control, as the islanders had known perfectly well that they'd likely be cut off sometime during the winter and had prepared for it. (Like my late mother-in-law, who saw a man lying un- conscious in the street, rushed into a nearby liquor store for a bottle of brandy and pushed through the crowd which had meanwhile gathered to the side of the victim, only to be told by the cop who had arrived on the scene that he'd had enough of that already, lady.) On the other hand, what was really important was the moment of contact. (The world is better because of my mother-in-law's concern, and I'm sure the man would have been touched by her action if he'd been sober enough.) The realities of isolation can be scary and so such efforts are appreciated, even though help may not be needed at that exact moment.

As the days close down into winter, changes in attitude occur. Harold and Elthea Turner live a couple of miles out of town, and it happened once that both Harold and the Barters, who live in the only house between them and town, were off-island at the same time. Elthea said that she hadn't thought herself particularly bothered by this until she noticed that she was being unusually careful about knives, and that she didn't want to chop the ice off the back steps. The concern is justified: Frank Barton lived alone on Kimball's Island in the winter during the fifties. Every few days he'd row the hundred yards across the Thoroughfare to buy groceries and visit; he returned from such a trip to Kimball's one day right before a cold spell, and Miss Lizzie didn't happen to see him walking around over there, as she usually did at various regular times, for the next three days. She got worried and asked Stanley Dodge to go over; he found Mr. Barton lying dead of a heart attack in the snow on the path to the house with the groceries he'd bought three days before strewn beside his body.

The missionary boat made the trip I've mentioned in the winter of 1943, in the middle of the war, so there probably was a special need for mail delivery. However, in this country there is a tradition of sanctity attached to the delivery of the U.S. MAIL which doesn't seem to be justified by its contents on the average day. After all that hardship and bravery, what is finally delivered could be five bills and a postcard from a friend in Florida telling you how warm it is down there, which you might just as soon have floating around in the bay gradually sinking. On the other hand, as there are no phones, the mail does assume a special importance.

Just as it is important in the usual ways, mail delivery is a rationale and a form of subsidy for regular public transportation. The contract for the transportation of the Island's mail is granted by the government to a private boat owner and so the mailboat traditionally has been the most practical small passenger boat, designed for other purposes but used for this. Nowadays, at least in the winter when there are fewer people traveling back and forth, this means a lobster boat. Before there were two-way radios, when the mailboat couldn't get through the pack ice in the winter, the Island was completely out of touch, with all the consequences to safety and convenience which that implies. When the bay froze solid the whole seven miles across to the Main, people would walk over on the ice, someone going ahead with a stick to test the patches which were dark and which might be thin. Salt-water ice has been characterized as tough as long as it stays cold, sometimes bending under the weight of a man but not breaking, but walking for any distance over it has never been common enough on the Maine coast for an expertise to develop, and it must have been pretty dangerous business.

In the thirties, Harold Turner's father, Charles, ran the mailboat, and the situations which were described in the newspaper articles I've quoted seemed to have been pretty common; the Island remained in contact with the mainland most of the time through sheer logistic ingenuity. The waters around the Island, fed by the fresh water flowing into it, would freeze first, and so the mailboat would get as close as possible and then everyone would walk, carrying on sleds the mail and the supplies they had gotten on the Main. When the Thoroughfare was filled with impenetrable pack ice, Captain Turner would go around to the northeast side of the Island and get as close to the shore there as he could— which sometimes was a mile out—and everyone would walk over the solid ice there to the shore. Moore's Harbor has always stayed ice-free because of a combination of tidal current and exposure to the southwest wind, but the road to it in the thirties was not passable in the winter, and so Harold, who was helping his father, would get up at four-thirty and drive from the east side to town, pick up the mail and any passengers and drive back to another cove on the eastern shore which, like Moore's Harbor, was almost always ice-free and so used by the mailboat.

In those days, winter trips were not to be taken lightly. According to an account by Floyd Rich, on New Year's Day of 1918 there was no open water to be seen between the Island and the Main from the top of Mount Champlain, the five-hundred-foot peak near the northern end of the Island, and he had to get back to school on the mainland. The next day a narrow passage had opened up across the top of the bay, but by then the mailboat was frozen in at the town landing. Floyd and a few other scholars set out in Charles Hamilton's twenty-six-foot fishing boat to meet the steamer which traveled across the top of the bay to serve the coastal towns. The interception was made and (the account continues)

I can still see Charles Hamilton with the then slight form of Gladys Bowen in his arms as he stood with one foot on the deck of our boat and the other on the guard rail of the steamer, and all the while the two boats were being separated farther and farther by the waves. Crew men from the steamer grabbed them both before they should be dunked in the icy water of the Bay and pulled them over the rail.

The fishing boat maneuvered to the lee side of the steamer for the rest of its passengers to transfer.

The word "dunked" implies something a little more light and playful than falling into water that cold between two boats. John Cousins was loading a heavy battery into a lobster boat a couple of winters ago and slipped and fell in; this had never happened to him before, and he said he suddenly understood how the shock and then the numbing might make it impossible to stay afloat after a matter of seconds.

What was new to my experience of winter was the combination of the cold and the sea; winter phenomena transformed the familiar environment of the summer. The winter equivalent of fog, which occurs on the coldest mornings, is called vapor and consists of either light wisps of condensation scudding close to the surface of the water or clouds as dense or denser than summer fog but which only extend to a distance of twenty or thirty feet in the air. A part of the condition for fog is the conjunction of cold water (the temperature of the Gulf of Maine ranges in the fifties in the summer) and warmer air; in winter, the combination is opposite: cold air meeting water which gets down to thirty but which still is warmer than the air.

Despite the mildness of the recent past there could be a series of severe winters starting any time, and although people nowadays are aware of the emergency help available in the form of two-way radio transmission and helicopters, the signs of oncoming winter are watched more carefully than they would be on the mainland. One day in October we got a letter from Virginia MacDonald saying that winter "doesn't feel very far away, it's blowed hard for a week and the men haven't been able to haul and tonight it feels more like November," and had we heard the prediction of heavy snow in December and a huge storm in February with accumulations to fifty inches? No—here in the isolation of New York we hadn't, but on the Island the reality of winter still exists as more than a subject of conversation.

The ownership of the mailboat and the mail-carrying contract which goes along with it resides on the Main, as does the regular captain. In any season, for a number of reasons, this is a bad arrangement, but in the winter it is intolerable, as there must be a boat available in case of emergency. By midwinter, all of the lobster boats would be hauled up except for Jack MacDonald's, and he would be out scalloping on many days, making it unavailable as a means of emergency transportation. Therefore, the mail run was taken over by Harold Turner, and the boat was kept at the Island in between trips.

Although people get up before six out of long habit, and, in the fall and spring, anyone who was hauling would be out by then, the day's beginning seems to be built around two events, the start of school at seven-forty-five and the departure of the mailboat at eight. I would hear Harold's car go by our house (a pleasant thing to rely on if I wanted to go over to the Main and couldn't get my car started) on his way down to the post office to pick up the sack of outgoing mail and chat with Miss Lizzie and anyone else who happened to have stopped by there after breakfast. The twenty-five-foot lobster boat, named simply after the Island and never known as anything but the mailboat, would be lying alongside the one winter float on the town dock which had been left in the water and which could stay unless the ice in the Thoroughfare got really bad (which it didn't that winter). Harold would squirt a little ether into the carburetor to give the engine the goose necessary to start up, and light the propane heater in the wheelhouse. Once the mailboat had cast off, the morning's passengers would stay in this small enclosure for the forty-minute ride, except for the idiotic photographer, who kept opening and closing the door, letting the cold in, as he rushed out onto the freezing afterdeck to photograph ducks and back in to get warm. As I found out after I relaxed a bit, it was a good place to chat and, along with the store and the post office, provided one of the Island's information centers. The fact that you had to speak up over the noise of the engine didn't hurt the easy conversational pace, and I learned a lot on those trips. The cabin also functions as an informal border check, as the trip is long and the cabin cozy, and it's pretty difficult not to divulge the minimum information about why you're coming on or going off, even though nobody asks, being habitually reluctant to pry.

The mailboat arrived at the Main about eight-forty-five and would return at ten-thirty, allowing an hour and a half for shopping, errands, mainland business and the pickup of the mail. The schedule was loose, and the boat would wait for any passengers who meant to be on the return trip. The fare was $1.50 per person, and the extra round trip Julie and I occasionally had to take when we arrived by plane in the middle of the day and wanted to go out that same day cost fifteen dollars.

By May there were enough fishing boats back in the water to provide emergency transportation, and the mailboat reverted to its regular command and was kept on the Main. Instead of the one round trip originating from the Island, there were three originating from the Main.

(In July and August, when the traffic picks up dramatically, the atmosphere of the trip is completely different. Our first summer, there was a new mailboat, designed specially for passengers and capable of carrying forty people, which it often did in August when the day trippers started to come on. It wasn't a bad-looking boat, and its fat lines, roof-covered open afterdeck and foolish fake

smokestack made it look flippant and summery, but I still boycotted it snob-
bishly; I had my own boat in the water, and anyway I didn't want to dilute my
fond memories of the winter boat.)

The first winter I spent about one week out of five on the Island, sometimes
with Julie and sometimes alone. The process of getting there involved a number
of transitions which could be quite abrupt. In the winter the plane service to the
nearby city was such that I would have to stay at a hotel overnight before going
to the Main, two hours by car away, to catch the morning mailboat to the Island.
Even with the hotel stay, the time of transit seemed ridiculously short; how
could I possibly get from the environment of the middle of New York City to the
environment of the Island in less than a week of acclimatization? I would be
driven from either the hotel or the plane to the Main by one of the Cousins
family—either Mary or her daughter-in-law Liz, who usually brought along one
or more of the kids. The fact that the Cousinses regularly spent the weekends
down on the Island made me feel that I'd skipped several stages of the trip and
that I'd stepped off the plane right into the life of the place. But I hadn't; there
were interesting problems like where to leave the good pants and jacket which
I needed to eat dinner in the hotel dining room but which I didn't want to carry
to the Island.

In the fall when I still had my own boat in the water, the transition was even
weirder. The airline schedule and the time of sunset worked out in such a way
that, coming in on the only available daily flight, I could *just* get out to the
Island by dark. I would step out of the environment of the airplane, which required nothing of me in the way of responsibility, having whisked me a thousand miles by magic, into the Cousinses' car, which I didn't even have to drive,
and then into the sixteen-foot Whaler, in which all by myself I'd have to get
seven miles out to sea in what weather conditions I didn't know and which had
seemed ridiculous to try to imagine earlier that day back in the middle of New
York. It was a jump in degree of responsibility, in clothing and, generally, in
states of being which boggled the mind—mine at least.

On the trip I made in November, sunset was about four o'clock, and I had
figured the logistics from the arrival of the plane through the trip to the Main,
through getting the boat started and loaded up and out to the Island down to
the minute; there was little margin for error and certainly no waiting for a
"fair chance." The error for which I'd left no margin came in the form of fog,
which I'd seen covering the coast from Boston north, but I was so driven to get
to the Island that I actually set off with Julie in a great rush from the boatyard
where we kept the Whaler into the rapidly deepening murk of the evening. At

the buoy just outside the harbor I luckily realized that I was emotionally back in New York and turned around, only to spend the next half hour bumping around from one unfamiliar wharf to another until I found a place to tie up for the night. It was like being out in the snow in your bedroom slippers. We called John and Liz Cousins, they fed us and put us up for the night, and we went out the next morning when my sensibility of where we really were and my common sense had caught up with us, like mislaid baggage.

The house we had rented for the winter sat on a wooded bluff overlooking Rich's Cove, on the east side of the Island. It was of log-cabin construction and was built in the twenties by Leon Small (the man who built our driftwood porch rocking chairs and who had built a number of similar summer cabins) for the late Fred Hoskins, a distinguished Congregational minister, who, among other accomplishments, had been a leader in the world ecumenical movement. His son, Ted, had been the Island summer minister for five years and the Island schoolteacher the year before. Dr. Hoskins' widow, Alice, who lived in the house in the summer, plays the church organ every Sunday in the summers and leads a choir in a town in Connecticut in the winter. She is an expert and passionate naturalist (her family claims that she is incapable of judging the length of anything—a boat, say—which is too large to be measured in chickadee wing flaps). She has that combination of gentleness and enthusiasm which is often associated with amateur naturalists (birdwatchers) and, underneath, a nice amount of strength, which is not supposed to go with the type. I liked her from the beginning and I would have liked her husband—which was important to living in their house all winter.

Through October, we slept out on her enclosed porch, which has the kind of view you would climb several hours to see. Looking out over the mouth of Rich's Cove as far to the east as could be seen, we had an open prospect uncommon to the Maine coast, where the view out to sea is usually stopped by an island or two. The reference point of the enormous scale of what you were looking at was more the sense of your own size than anything else, as when you stand on a mountaintop. Looking out over a period of time we were aware of the variety within the same general frame, as the light, the weather and the season changed.

When my uncovered nose got particularly cold one morning, and Julie wasn't around to bolster my resistance, I retreated into the kitchen, which we had picked out to isolate into winter quarters. The source of heat consisted of two kerosene burners set in a stove whose oven ranges burned propane—the usual arrangement on the Island. It worked fairly well, although I continually worried that a sudden rise in temperature would flood the burner with kerosene despite the thermostat's control. This only happened once and didn't produce any damage. As I said earlier, Maurice Barter had enclosed the kitchen walls in plastic, and I had nailed strips of tarpaper along the piles which raised that part of the house above the ground and piled pine boughs against the walls elsewhere. We weather-stripped the door leading from the kitchen to a kind of pantry-shed off it and the door between the kitchen and the rest of the house. We laid insulated metal foil and a carpet over the floor and halfway up the walls, and that, along with the aluminum foil we draped around the leaky stovepipe to deflect the soot, made the kitchen look like a slightly rundown discothèque.

As well as the cooking part of the stove, the heater in the bathroom and a few lights were fueled by propane, which was stored in tanks outside the house. There was a propane refrigerator, but starting in November we just left perishables in mouse-proof containers outside the door of the heated kitchen in the shed. By then, we had become a snug oasis in the middle of the winter world of several small animals. There was a squirrel who kept hanging around the back door, not for the excess vegetables I'd occasionally throw out but in order to attempt bold dashes into the shed, where the garbage was kept, and, hopefully, into the warm kitchen. We had a few resident mice, who would come out to play noisily in the middle of the night with any paper they could find. If something like that had happened in the city I'd have been disgusted, but here I was just mildly annoyed and went back to sleep.

Our water was pumped from the well by motor to a storage tank, raised on a platform next to the house. By the November trip the temperature was below freezing often enough to require that the tank and the pipes be drained, and we embarked on the condition of no interior plumbing—which is to say, *real* winter. We had prepared for this, but I think it's impossible for people who have lived all their lives in a city to absorb fully the consequences of living in a house without running water, even if they have camped a lot. You'd realized that the absence of interior plumbing meant consequence A, consequence B, and maybe on through G, but, my God, you hadn't realized that it meant you couldn't do H. Consequence H for me was the prohibition against allowing the smallest amount of water to go down the drain, as it would freeze and expand.

The well was about fifty yards from the house, and I found to my surprise that we used only two gallons of water a day, including minimal bathing. It was an adventure going to it at night, because I'd almost inevitably get scared out of my wits by the loud angry snort of one of the deer which hung around in abundance. I also had the frightening fantasy of slipping and falling into the well and being unable to get out and being too far inside for my shouts to be heard. I was going to hang a rope down into it until I realized that people had been going to wells in winter for a long time and that if I was careful and didn't do too much solitary drinking I *wouldn't* fall in. This is called confidence gained from the experience of wilderness.

Among the consequences I *had* realized was the matter of the toilet. We had isolated the kitchen from the rest of the house as well as from the outside, and the only other room we used was the bathroom, where we kept the chemical toilet. This is a jolly arrangement, consisting of a pail surrounded by a toilet seat and what is meant to suggest the tank of a regular toilet. The heart of the matter is the "pine"-scented fluid which is mixed with water and poured into the pail. The fact that this is a deadly poison, combined with the neurotic results of imperfect toilet training in my childhood, served to drive me out of doors to a cold but friendly fallen tree trunk in all but extreme cold or gloom of night. The chemical toilet was emptied into the septic tank, and I think that covers *that* part of my winter experience.

Outside the range of the power company's electrification, all of the winter houses had generators to provide current for lights, television and most appliances, including washing machines. Ours was used only for light, and it was located in a shed out the back door. There was a switch inside the house which operated the starter, but in the middle of the winter it seemed a little high-handed to think that any machine was going to star as remotely as that. Every late afternoon, after performing the gas and oil ceremony, I went to the mat with the generator, and, unlike certain cars I could mention, it only failed me once and that was when it was fifteen below. There would be the lovely sound of the one-cylinder motor catching, and the wintry night would be filled with comforting noise and light, just like home.

I'd gone out to do this one evening in October at the exact moment when a late-visiting summer resident arrived at the front door of the house to invite me to dinner and, getting no reply to her knock, entered. She was a little nervous anyway, as she thought I was someone she had known in the past but wasn't sure, and, as she sneaked into the dark house calling out tentative greetings, all of a sudden the generator started up and all the lights went on. She was startled, which served her right for sneaking up on hermits. The noise of the generator was particularly loud then, as the water cistern into which the exhaust pipe led, muffling the sound, had crumbled. Later, the fifteen-year-old son of a plumbing contractor from the Main who spends weekends on the Island, with typical ingenuity, scavenged a muffler from one of the derelicts around his house and put it on, bringing relative quiet to the nights around Rich's Cove. Even so, it seemed like a lot of noise for five one-hundred-watt bulbs, but it was welcome.

The year-round daily schedule of most people on the Island was one which

I admire in the abstract but which, despite serious attempts, I've never been able to follow for more than a little time. Those who were going out to haul got up at about four-thirty so as to be out in their boats by five-thirty. Otherwise, almost everybody got up around five, so that by mailboat time at eight the Island was well into its day. Dinner was at noon, and suppertime varied between five and six—six for fishermen who had hauled that day, as they weren't finished until then, but five for the others. This meant that there was a relaxed evening period of two or three hours before the usual bedtime of nine o'clock. In the light of a summer evening, this was when there would be ballgames, and it was always visiting time; "Come on over after supper" generally meant sometime around five-thirty. In some parts of Europe this is the time of the promenade, and there was the same easiness about this period of early evening on the Island except that the communal activity took place indoors, where everyone more or less held open house. If your car was sick, this is when you would go and see Harold van Doren, whose evenings were less relaxed as a result. From May to November Phil Alley and Carol and Gordon Chapin provided the other exception to this general Island routine by tending their herring weir in the evenings and into the night. As for me, I was busy covering my own experience and photographing out of doors in the late-afternoon light most of the time so that we didn't eat until after dark.

By the time full winter arrived I had heard about the feeling of isolation and anticipated a kind of hibernation. I figured that in the long winter evenings, which start about four o'clock, I'd be able to get the reading done which I'd intended to do all year. Actually, that winter I read no more than five pages of one of the many books I'd brought, and I would return to New York exhausted from the round of social activities which were piled on top of photographing and note compiling. As an example, I'll describe one week. Julie and I arrived on the Island on Sunday, January 9, and, although there was the usual round of daytime visiting, we spent that night and Monday night at home. On Tuesday, we had supper with Pat and Annie Haynes and spent the evening learning "83" from them in preparation for Men's Card Night on Wednesday; this is a complicated pinochle-type card game played on the Maine coast which turns out to be well beyond the limits of my sense of mathematical order. Ladies' Card Party that week was to take place after Julie had left, so there was no chance for her to make up for my density. Men's Card Party was at Bill and Bernadine Barter's; there were, unfortunately, just enough with me for two tables of play, and everyone was very kind.

Thursday night was volleyball in the town hall auditorium, at which I was better, but not much; the transformation of the town hall had been accomplished, under Bernadine Barter's leadership, by stringing a net across the hall, tying the hanging lights to one side and buying a volleyball on the Main. Participants in the winter volleyball series generally included about twelve of the grownups and all of the kids. It wasn't what you'd call first-class volleyball, but it got the old circulation going, particularly as the town hall is unheated in the winter and most of us were held down by heavy clothing; Bill Barter played in his fishing boots. After volleyball that night, I watched Truffaut's *Jules and Jim* on Pat and Annie's TV. I go to the movies a lot in New York but hardly watch television at all, and so it was a strange mixture of experiences to go from absorption in this film, which is an old favorite of mine, out into the unlit night of the winter Island and back to light the propane lamps (it was too late to start the generator) in our winterized kitchen. The reality of the good film and the reality of my life on the Island, when juxtaposed, became two fantasies.

On Friday night Harold and Olive van Doren gave a party, to which it seemed everyone had been invited and most had come. The trailer was crowded, a couple of bottles were opened and we danced to Olive's collection of records, inhibited only by the lack of space. It was a gathering of people who had been seeing each other regularly over the last few years, so the party didn't have the air of a reunion. It reminded me of an office party without any of the pressure of trying to impress the boss, get one up on a colleague or seduce the secretary. Everybody was easy with everyone, old subjects of gentle teasing were trotted out (Maurice Barter's refusal to dance, the latest disaster in my car fleet, and so on), familiar stories and opinions were reaffirmed. Simply, there was a joy in each other's company, a celebration of the present fact that most of us were crowded into one small enclosed space. At least, that was the way it seemed to me.

The word got around—mostly at Harold and Olive's party—that Bill Stevens, the ranger, who was working for the power company that winter, was going to put his iceboat together on Sunday afternoon, so about eight of us arrived at the end of the pond in the bright, bitter cold of the early afternoon the next day. It wasn't a gathering of the gang at the old familiar skating pond, complete with bonfire, because the long expanse of ice and the cold were on too impressive a scale for it to be anything but a foray into the wilderness which lay all around us on the Island. There were eight adults and three kids, and we skated shakily around and assembled the iceboat, in which Bill Stevens and Pat Tully then set off down the pond, running before the wind; Pat and Annie Haynes and I set off after them, drawn by the jib, which they hadn't been able to rig. For more than a mile we skimmed over the smooth surface, our skates bouncing

on the occasional patches of rough surfaces; I'd forgotten that there was that
much ice to skate on in one spot in the whole world. Bill and Bernadine Barter
had driven their truck down to the other end, and so we didn't have to skate
back. We stopped off at Pat and Donna Tully's to warm up, talking generally,
while Pat, Bill and Harold van Doren tried to figure out improvements to the
iceboat. That night I packed to go back to New York and started to catch up on
my notes.

Just as there was a luxury in having two miles of frozen pond to skate down,
there was the luxury of having all that spectacular space available to the hand-
ful of us who were inclined to wander about in it. Having known the coast
only in the summer, I felt the emptiness of the houses and the absence of boats
in the coves. However, this wasn't the feeling of living in a ghost town, perhaps
because I knew the houses would be occupied in the summer, but also because
by that time I felt that the Island really belonged to the winter residents, and
that we had expanded our individual spheres to fill the rich emptiness. Walking
around the elegance of the empty Point "cottage" complex, looking in through
windows at the paraphernalia of summer lives, left casually as if the house had
no existence outside of the summer, I felt the childish pleasure of wandering
around in this garden of riches without having to say hello to the grownups.
The summer houses were doll houses, which we could look into but couldn't
enter because we were the wrong size—or maybe because we had come from
another planet. Boom Beach in the winter was strange and beautiful, unknown
(I felt) to any but a few of us and therefore all ours. There is a sense of power
which goes along with custodianship.

There were strange juxtapositions. One afternoon I was on the porch of the
most impressive of the Point houses, looking out at the empty Thoroughfare
and the silent town, when the sonic boom from a jet shattered the air and sent
all the gulls up screaming into the air for nearly ten minutes. I expected to hear
sirens or that someone would at least ring the church bell to protest this intrusion.

The winter population is small and is located on the northeast corner, in
town, and scattered along one section of the east side, and so there is a large
part of the Island which goes unvisited, in which all kinds of things can go on
without notice. In the early spring we went down to the pond and found a
plane, which had brought in a couple of ice fishermen from the mainland. At
first I thought they had a hell of a nerve, but then I realized that they had a
perfect legal and moral right to land and fish, the surface of the lake being in
the public domain even though surrounded by privately owned land—just as

no property owner can stop you from traveling on a stream unless your canoe capsizes and you are forced to stand on the private property of the stream bed. People on the Island knew about them and didn't resent their visits at all. The pilot had spent a good deal of time adapting the plane to land on the ice, doing all the work himself and using the head of a shovel to make a tail skid. I admit that the fact of this elegant improvisation alone meant that he could do no wrong as far as I was concerned. They had caught few brook trout and a number of fresh-water smelts by the time we arrived, using the standard ice-fishing techniques of connecting the minnow-baited hook and line, dangled through a hole in the ice, to a spring arrangement which would trip when the bait was taken and the fish hooked, causing the little flag on the end of the spring to fly up.

Small-plane travel among the Maine islands has been increasing in the past ten years. As the cost of operating a small plane becomes less, the cost of flying becomes feasible for other than millionaires. There is one island about twenty miles away and far out to sea where most of the fishermen fly to the mainland rather than going in their own boats or the mailboat. There is an enormous saving of time, and the fishermen on this particular island can take advantage of it, as they are wealthier than most, due to the fact that they fish in remote waters which can be protected from competition. We flew out there a few years ago with the bush pilot who serves them and most of the area. He's a good flier—so good in fact that the Sunday we left there were a number of fishermen gathered around the landing strip on their day off to watch him bring his plane in through a ceiling of fog which hung about thirty feet off the ground. I got the impression that they weren't there to pick up the pieces but to watch a piece of expertise which wasn't too different from what they did in their own boats. In a way, bush pilots on the Maine coast have gathered around them a tradition of mastery associated with the old sea captains.

In terms of isolation, the years of World War II must have been like a four-year winter. The young men were away, the rationing of gasoline made travel difficult, there were almost no summer people. What must have been most isolating, however, was the fact that the coast of Maine was right in the middle of the war zone. This was not known at the time, as disclosure might have caused panic, but it's remarkable to me that so few people know even now the extent of German activity along the coast. Of course, there were the submarines. The mother of a friend of mine was sitting at a Washington dinner party in the early fifties next to a member of the diplomatic staff of the Federal Republic; she mentioned conversationally that she had spent most of her summers on the Maine coast, and he replied that to him, also, this coast was one of the most beautiful in the world. She remarked that he had told her earlier in the conversation that this was his first trip to the United States, and after a moment of confusion he explained that he had served on a U-boat during the war. All along the coast U-boats would occasionally surface alongside fishing boats, take their gas and perhaps a few lobsters and submerge. The crews landed on some of the more remote islands down east and did calisthenics. Spies were landed: there is an island near where we used to spend our summers on which there is a well-built shack set on a platform and so skillfully camouflaged by the trees between it and the shore that it can hardly be seen from the water, even close by; when you move a few branches, this shack commands an excellent view of the bay. A couple of Germans were landed from a submarine which was able to come right alongside the island in the hundred-foot-deep water right off the shore, and reported the comings and goings of the North Atlantic Fleet for several months before they were discovered.

The Island, also, had its share of wartime activity. One of the summer houses on the east side was occupied for several days by German spies, who are presumed to have been signaling information about the traffic of warships in and out of a nearby port to a submarine lying offshore. The events which led to their detection are Hitchcockesque: two children were walking by the house, which had been empty for over a year, and saw a curtain move. They reported this to adults, who, evidently, didn't believe them soon enough to prevent the escape of the spies: that night some fishermen, who were camping on York Island near the water they were then hauling, heard the rare sound of a boat with an outboard motor go by in the fog, heading straight out to sea, and then suddenly stop well before it had gotten out of earshot. Too late, some of the men investigated and found evidence of the invasion, including a rubber boat which the spies had used for coming ashore and had left when they were picked up by the mysterious motorboat. I understand that the dinghy was in plain view on the beach, and it would probably have been seen if, as in a normal year, there had been any summer people, who tend to wander around more than the year-round residents.

The meeting between Roosevelt and Churchill which created the Atlantic Charter took place on a destroyer not far from the Island. Just as now, it was a tucked-away place in the middle of things.

As well as all the other things I've mentioned, the Island is a body of safety surrounded by danger. The sea is too cold, even in summer, to allow any more than a few minutes of life in it, and therefore most people don't know how to swim—even the fishermen. Drowning occurs fairly regularly on the coast, and the Island draws death from the sea around it as well as sustenance. A press clipping from 1900:

Two Promising Young Men, Another Just Escaped a Like Fate

Herman Coombs aged 20, and Gustus Rich, aged 13 years, were drowned at
Moore's Harbor at this place Tuesday, Dec. 4 at about 5 P.M., and Freeman Hamilton,
who was with them, was just alive when rescued by Prentiss Phinney and Mr.
Moore. The cause of their sad accident was from hauling a lobster car on a small
boat.

    The smack Kingfisher, Capt. Chas. Rich, had been at Duck Harbor after lobsters.
Freeman Hamilton, who lives there, came up to Moore's Harbor in the smack.
Herman Coombs and his brother Albert went aboard and got a dip net to bail their
lobsters out of the car with, Albert stayed aboard of the smack, and Freeman
Hamilton and Capt. Rich's son, Gustus, went with Herman after the lobsters.
The car being small, they could not bail it with the dip net, so they thought they
would haul the car on the boat. They got it on all right, when Herman's fingers
and feet both slipped and he fell on the side of the boat, causing the car to slip
about half way off, where it caught and upset the boat. It being dark, no one saw
them, Prentiss Phinney and Mr. Moore heard them hollering, but thought at
first that they were going off to the smack joking each other as they usually do,
but as they continued to holler, they went out to see what the matter was. It was
then so dark that they could not see them, but could hear them in the water. When
they got their boat off and got there, Freeman Hamilton was the only one left
and he was about to give up.

    I showed this clipping to a friend, and she was reminded of the term "rites of
passage," which refers to the formal ceremonies accompanying the transition
from one age group to another—for example, from childhood to adolescence
and from adolescence to youth. Thirteen-year-old Gustus was doing a man's
job, going off joking with the men into the December night. At the same age,
and according to similar rites, a Masai boy is sent out to kill his first lion, which
sometimes kills him. I wonder if the death is easier, having been formally prepared for, or coming without warning; the cold water must have felt different
to Gustus than he had ever imagined it would, as it broke in on the warmth of
his successful initiation into the world of working men. The danger is not really
acknowledged on the Maine coast; hauling alone, the lobsterman figures maybe
he'll put a knife on the afterdeck so that he'll have a chance to grab it as he's
hauled over the side with his foot tangled in the warp of a trap he's setting,
but he doesn't, depending (maybe wisely) on the multitude of precautions
which have so far prevented that from happening.

    Dying is a descent into loneliness, among other things, and drowning must
be particularly so, because being saved generally depends on the arrival of peo-

ple who, if they only arrive in time, can effect the rescue—as opposed to fire, where a bunch of people can arrive in time and yet not be able to enter the building. There must be that moment when the drowning man can see the house on the shore or the boat just out of reach; he is surrounded by people *just* out of reach, who are *almost* enough aware of his predicament. In the early part of the century Leon Small's father, Albert, was drowned just off the east side coast when the boom of his peapod knocked him overboard as he was raising sail. At least, this is the way people figure he drowned, as the peapod was found drifting with the sail down and the halyard unloosened, and Mr. Small's body came ashore near the Seal Rocks. Leon Small said he'd seen his father's body carried up the beach in a dream he'd had shortly before the accident, and Les Grant down at Head Harbor thought he remembered just barely hearing a cry for help as he stood outside his house that day; his house is well out of voice range from the nearest point that Albert Small's boat could have been, but adrenaline might have pushed the cry further and the psychic adrenaline of the Island might have reached out beyond the usual limits of reception to receive it.

A great many doctors started to come to the Island as summer residents in the early fifties, so that by now there is all kinds of medical talent at hand during July and August, but for most of the year there is no doctor nearer than the Main. This was the case the year round before the fifties, but Miss Lizzie asserts that only one person ever died on the Island for want of a doctor, and that was long ago—so long ago, in fact, that she can't remember who it was, having been told about it as a girl.

There was a Dr. Noyes who came down from the Main on house calls during the thirties, often in response to signal flares set by Clarence Turner. The flares would have saved the time of a trip to the Main to summon him, as there were no radios then. Until the fifties there was a Dr. Brown who would make house calls, but mostly the Island has a tradition of home remedies and midwifery. The last baby born on the Island, in the fifties, was delivered by Polly Bowen, a nurse who came from Head Harbor and who was on the Island at the time, but Miss Lizzie was brought into the world in 1893 by a Mrs. Bennett, a neighbor skilled in midwifery, who delivered her eight siblings as well. Miss Lizzie's arrival cost three dollars, which Phil Alley remembers is what he cost twenty-five years later in his birthplace on the mainland; it's a tribute to Maine fairness that it didn't cost more on the Island, whose isolation from medical attention made the job riskier. Miss Lizzie also recalled that all the nine children in her family (she counted their names to make sure of the number) had later had the measles at the same time; that one of her teeth, as well as many of her neighbors', had been hauled by Haskell Turner, in one of the moments when he wasn't shoeing horses or making elegant ornamental ironwork; and that the islanders used to sew up each other's sometimes severe wounds with needle and thread (ordinary needle and thread—not sailmaker's, which would have been too heavy).

Now that house calls are a thing of the past and methods of transportation faster, a medical emergency means a fast trip to the nearest hospital on the mainland. There is a regional ambulance service based on the Main (to which the Island is regularly the highest per capita contributor of all the towns involved), but in certain instances it is handier to use the first transportation which comes to hand. In '64 Dennis Eaton had an accident which severed an artery; Harold Turner, who was near at hand, stopped the bleeding at a pressure point, hailed Stanley Dodge, who happened to be passing by in his car, drove with him to town and started off in the mailboat to the Main. It was midday, when few CB radios are normally turned on, but luckily Harold's son Dick had his on and met the boat at the dock with his car. It is twenty-eight miles from there to the hospital, and Harold claims they made it in sixteen minutes, which would make an average speed of 105 miles per hour. The doctor said it was just as well they got him there when they did, as he had lost two quarts of blood and had about ten minutes to go. A margin of ten minutes is pretty slight for a trip from the middle of an island seven miles out to sea to a hospital thirty miles inland from the coast, requiring three forms of transportation.

When there was a heart attack on the Island a few years ago, Harold made the trip to the Main in the middle of the night in a thick of fog, and he says he didn't see anything from the time he left the Island until he saw the lights on the dock at the Main.

Miss Lizzie fell and broke her hip one winter evening in 1966, when she was seventy-three. She was tending to her dog in the back room of the post office, and she says she must have turned around funny; it was past the time when there would have been anyone coming in, and for the next hour she inched her way along the fifteen feet from the back room to below the shelf where the CB radio sat, raised herself up and managed to call Stan Dodge, who lives about fifty yards down the road. It so happened that most of the younger men were off-island just then, but by chance the men from a game-management team which had been tagging deer on the Island were nearby, and they helped carry Miss Lizzie, tied into an armchair, down the gangway, which was steeply inclined as it was low tide, to the float and onto the mailboat. Just as they set out a snowstorm started.

It's incidents like these which, after a while, must make for a condition of constant preparedness; along about the second day of a snowstorm or as the ice packs in during a cold spell, people must begin to wonder what they would do if they had to get someone to the mainland fast, and they must subconsciously prepare for such an eventuality. Therefore there is a totally accepted rule that there will be at least one boat in the Thoroughfare, if not all the time, then at least most of every day, and certainly every night. There are enough helicopters around by now, but they're a lot more limited by weather than a lobster boat in competent hands.

The biggest threat to the Island is fire. Most of the trees are pine, filled with inflammable sap and joined by interlocking roots just under the surface of the ground, along which fire can spread undetected. For a long time after a fire, watches have to be maintained against the persistence of this underground smoldering. (Harold Turner can remember an evening after the 1949 fire on the east side which he spent with Governor Bradford of Massachusetts, a summer resident, who speculated a little bit on the political consequences of his constituency's finding out that he had spent the night preparing to put out a fire with a chamber pot full of water.) In any bad fire on the mainland the local equipment can be augmented by equipment from neighboring towns, but on an island this is impossible and a large fire now would be fought by helicopter lift, which would take a long time to organize.

At the base of the concern is the realization that the Island is a limited area completely surrounded by very cold water. This would seem like a nightmare fantasy were it not for the actuality of the 1949 Bar Harbor fire, which cut off that town and forced the fairly sizable population down to the town dock with its back to the November sea. A Dunkerque-like evacuation had started, and there was worry that there might not be enough time to get everyone off before the fire reached them, when the wind suddenly changed its direction.

There is one fire engine on the Island, kept in a small garage in town and capable of pumping salt water as well as fresh, and there is a fire warden elected at every town meeting. My first year on, this was Pat Haynes, the teacher. The fire crew is anybody and everybody on the Island, there being no need for the formality of even a volunteer fire department. The alarm is the church bell. When a fire occurs, the Island seems to draw together and act with near-perfect efficiency, probably because everyone's been secretly planning what they would do and holding interior fire drills.

There is a tiny cabin on the shore north of Rich's Cove, commanding a wide view of the sea from the top of the bluff on which it is situated but separated by about a half mile of woods from any road. It belonged to Miss Ava, Miss Lizzie's late sister, and one of her young relatives who was camping in it emptied the ashes from the fireplace out the door one day without properly checking them, starting a fire in the brush in front of the cabin. A lobsterman working offshore a way saw the fire and ran his boat into Rich's Cove at full speed and up onto the mud shore at the head of the cove to give the alarm; although not an islander, he must have had a deep sense of the special dangers of fire, as well as being a pretty wonderful person, to do such a thing. Joe and Marion Williams, our summer landlord's children, were shingling the roof of the house, and he called to them. They ran to Miss Ava's house, a hundred yards away, and called Maurice Barter on the informal battery-operated "telephone" which he had rigged up to connect his aunt's house with his. Maurice jumped into his car and drove through town, blowing his horn, ran up to the church and rang the bell. He and the others who, hearing the church bell, had driven to town got the pumper started, drove as far as they could into Rich's Cove and carried the "portable" pump through the woods to the cabin, drew water from the sea at the bottom of the bluff and put the fire out before it had burned more than an acre. This happened in 1969, and it was the last fire of consequence on the Island.

The first reported fire on the Island occurred in the 1870s; it was the one which was started by blueberry pickers, and it burned for two months until the snow came, denuding the top of the ridge. There are no detailed reports, but I'd guess that people tried to contain it by firebreaks chopped out of the woods but that it kept breaking out as the fire traveled along the root systems of the pines. A pamphlet on the flora and fauna of the Island, which I found in the library, mentions a smaller fire at Duck Harbor in 1894. It was described to me by Gooden Grant, who is ninety-six and remembers being awakened by his father in the middle of the night while they were visiting a friend on a nearby large island with the alarm that the Island was burning up. He remembers sailing with his father across the bay in a strong easterly breeze on the hurried trip home that night and seeing what looked like his Island home burning. He describes burning trees flying up in the air as the fire reached them and traveling like huge torches to set other areas ablaze. It must have been quite an experience for a boy, sailing across the windy bay in the middle of the night— the kind of memory that lasts after seventy-eight years. In 1940 the kerosene stove in the Turners' house exploded; Harold Turner was nearby at Dennis Eaton's and heard the church bell rung by Elthea, who had driven to town. He realized from the direction of the smoke that it was his house. The whole place burned, and the town helped him build a new home.

6

COMMUNITIES WITHIN
THE ISLAND

There are four specific locations outside of town which could be said to have separate identities from the identity of the Island as a whole. The Point is the old summer colony, deserted in winter and separated physically (and, until the last couple of years, socially) from the rest of the Island. At Moore's Harbor there is a summer colony of five houses whose inhabitants have always had a more intimate connection with the year-round residents than the other summer people but who are tucked away physically from the Island proper. On the east side there is a loose aggregate of widely separated houses of year-round residents who consider themselves more connected with the Island as a whole than with any part of it. Then there are Rich's Cove and Head Harbor—two communities which are off by themselves a little bit and which, until very recently, had year-round populations and unique year-round subidentities. This isolation within the isolation of the Island is easier to understand when you consider that in the past sea travel was in many cases as fast as travel by the road, and an individual cove, being the place where a group of neighbors sheltered their boats, was the center of a separate small community. An account of summer life in 1917 indicates that a trip from Moore's Harbor to Rich's Cove represented a full day's outing to see old friends, who were visited surprisingly seldom when you consider that the places are three miles apart on the same island. The town, on the other hand, has always been the center of the Island and familiar to all.

We lived in Rich's Cove. Alice Hoskins' house, our winter home, sat on a small bluff overlooking the cove, as well as the open sea to the east. Our geographic orientation, however, was to the cove, and this is where we were impelled when, for example, we wanted to make a small excursion. All that winter, and even in the summer when we lived right down in it, Rich's Cove had the feel of a ghost town; more than that, it had the feel of a room which someone has *just* left—where someone has just gotten up from the rocking chair, which is still moving. It is partly inhabited in July and August and the evidence of the summer people lasts into the fall, but mostly the feeling comes from a sense of great year-round activity in the recent past. Starting down from our house on the bluff on our not unpleasantly haunted walks, we would first come to the house which Gene and Wynne Skolnikoff had bought from Leon Small. Behind that was William Rich's old house, now lived in during the summer only. Crossing the stream which emptied into the head of the cove, we would be in front of another summer residence, which had been built by Captain Charles Rich about 1885. Next was what was referred to by sentimental late-nineteenth-century Riches as "the old homestead," owned now by Ken and Beth Breeze, summer residents, and into which we would move in the summer. Up a meadow beyond the Breezes' was a cluster of houses, one of which had been lived in until recently by Miss Ava, Miss Lizzie's spinster sister, another by her brother Llewellyn and his wife, Mineola, and another which served as the store and residence of another brother, Sam. Passing through this cluster, the dirt road continued for a half mile on to the Old Cove, where John Rich, still another brother of Miss Lizzie's, had been building a new house for himself when he died in 1968. The entire point is laid bare of trees, and John Rich's unwalled house is covered with plastic.

The real, if not the official, caretaker of all of this still-warm richness of Rich's Cove is my friend and neighbor Maurice Barter. Maurice (pronounced Morris) is Miss Lizzie's nephew, the son of her late sister Clara, and the two of them and Maurice's wife, Helen, are the last of the Riches on the Island. His lobster boat and my ridiculous-looking big outboard were the only two boats in the cove all that summer. He keeps his traps and fishing gear in one of the last of the sound fish shacks which had been built and were used by his uncles, and every time I saw him walking by our house on his way to and from the dilapidated wharf, I imagined how strangely empty the cove must seem to him. When he was a boy his five fishermen uncles and the Smalls filled the place with life. Their unofficial, extralegally-held lobstering territory extended out from the mouth of the cove most of the way across to York Island and down York Narrows to its end, and they didn't have to go much farther to haul their livings. Lobstermen from the Main camped on York Island during the

summer, but they stayed outside of the line of ledges running down the middle of York Narrows. The fishing was good enough to sustain both groups in their own territories, and relations were generally friendly. They used to set hoop nets not far out in the cove, and practically every time the twine was drawn in tight around the mouth of one, a couple of bushels of flounder and sculpin would be hauled up. In winter they would spear flounder through the ice. When the herring were in, the summer nights would be lit up and the faces of the men blackened by the fire from the "dragon" torches on the bows of the peapods, as they shoveled in the herring with dip nets. The shacks near the wharf were in good repair, and there was one out on the wharf itself to serve the five or six fishermen. Into the cove came fifty-foot lobster smacks from the mainland ports to transport the Riches' lobsters in their sea-water wells. The oil boat would come in regularly to deliver gasoline and kerosene to the store, which was operated by Sam Rich. There were clambakes for forty and fifty people.

The bustle of the cove in Maurice's youth was the peak of an expansion which had been going on for three generations. The photograph above, taken before 1889 from right in front of the Breezes' house, shows the old wharf; lying in the cove are sloops belonging to Edwin, George and Stillman Rich; Stillman is shown down by the shed. The dory belongs to Albert Small, and the peapod, farthest out, to Albert and Willie Rich. The schooner off the point is the *Sarah Hyde,* a lobster smack, and, to judge from Mr. Rich's lack of concern, was a common sight. I can imagine my excitement if something as big as that, even in modern shape, came around the Point. Across the Narrows, York Island looks busy too.

In 1905, the "old homestead" down by the shore had been bought from Minerva, the widow of George Rich, by a summer resident—a lady named Della Champagne—and so the cove wasn't completely cut off from the summer community, or rather the summer community wasn't completely cut off from it. Mineola Rich, Llewellyn's wife, was the head housekeeper at the Point, which in those days must have been a position with as much responsibility as that of the butler of an English aristocratic household. Ava Rich was away most winters, working for various summer families in their Boston houses.

The layout of houses around the cove is a textbook example of beautiful site planning, although, of course, it wasn't consciously planned. Rather, from the beginnings of the settlement, each new house was built within a naturally formed rather than a man-decreed lot, taking advantage of the contour of the shoreline within the cove and the complicated little ravines which the ledges form as they stretch inland. The result is that the land from the water seems crowded with houses, a nice sight for a returning fisherman, while on shore each feels separate from the other. The cove is dominated by the land, into which the Riches and the Smalls set their houses and outbuildings with a grace which comes of deep familiarity.

The first to settle in the cove was Robert Douglas in 1802, and sometime after that he built the house in which we spent the summer. His daughter Eleanor married John Rich, and in 1844 he sold the property to his son-in-law, who began the line whose name will end on the Island with Miss Lizzie. Miss Champagne added the porch, but other than that the house has the same tucked-in quality which it had 150 years ago; I mean by "tucked-in" that when you're inside you *feel* inside, you feel sheltered, as a house is meant to make you feel. This is because the windows are small, but also because the rooms, in their shape and size, fit nicely around you.

Maurice says that in ten years of the late fifties and early sixties the place was cleaned out by death, and there were no children or newcomers. He hangs on. Like his uncles, he went lobstering, except for a short period when he lived in upstate New York and worked in a furniture factory, from which he returned to the Island. In the fifties a storm wiped out all but thirty of his two hundred traps and about that time the lobstermen from the Main, who were younger and more aggressive, began to move into York Narrows in strength. The productive territory which had been informally reserved to the Riches by the pressure of their presence could not be held by Maurice alone, and for the past two years or so he says he can hardly find a place to set a string of his own traps in among those of the mainland lobstermen. He has been fishing less and less, and the summer I was on he had trouble with his boat and didn't set out a single trap until August, and then only a few. The identification of the cove with the past seemed to be expressed clearly in his gentle bitterness, as he complained, only partly joking, of the people on the Main (*"Lord . . . you want to watch out for them fellows"*). It's not easy to watch your birthright vanish and, as one who himself is not easy with competition, I could understand his feelings.

"I don't know—I might just go to [a nearby city] if there's nothing to do here," he said more than once that year. Of course, there was always something to do, given the fact that Maurice is a skilled carpenter. After his work on the power company electric poles was finished in the spring, he started to work on an extensive remodeling job on the Skolnikoffs' house; most of the time, however, he exercises his old-fashioned compulsion to craftsmanship by carving boat models. The lobster boat he made that winter is not a model of any existing boat but rather the model of an ideal boat which Maurice would like to own; it doesn't represent a radical departure in design, but, as it grew out of the solid block of spruce (carefully selected so that the knots would fall in what would be the hollow of the afterdeck), he made little changes in the lines to conform to this personal ideal. He worked on it all winter, off and on but mostly on. In an earlier time it's possible that Maurice would have been able to do this work or work like it all the time, that his pace of work and attention to detail would not only have been appreciated but would have fit into a simpler economy. The amount of skill, understanding, experience and effort which went into the boat, exercised in the accomplishment of some result in the heyday of Rich's Cove—a boat model, a house or a lot of fish—would have been paid for; if a man put all of these things in, he would get out a living. Now, Maurice would have to have the proper marketing connections and the ability to meet abstract marketing conditions to make the beginnings of a living from major products like the boat model or the other smaller things he makes. Eager types like me bust in with all kinds of ideas for marketing things which he might make with less investment of time, and he was very open to such suggestions. But filling the order for two hundred handcrafted clamrollers by next Tuesday for the Christmas rush might be like being back at the furniture factory. I guess it takes a Medici to pay not only for art but for what was considered simply the product of common skill in an earlier time on the Island.

Helen Barter came to the Island as a girl, when her father, Harry Smith, took the job of keeping the lighthouse which is located at the southern, or seaward, entrance to the Thoroughfare on Robinson Point (named after Holbrook Robinson, who was the first lighthouse keeper). The light ran on kerosene then. It is still active, although unmanned, and runs on a combination of batteries and propane.

Helen remembers two things from her childhood in the lighthouse which are worthy of mention because they are so at variance with what seems to me to be the understated but still real welcome given by the Island to those who come to it. When the Smiths arrived on the Island in the middle of winter, the store was unexpectedly closed, as John K. Barter, who ran it, had had to go off-island for a few days. The family had arrived without supplies, and the first Island family whom they asked for help actually refused them. It could be that in the winters of those days people had only laid by enough for themselves, but it seems a harsh thing to have done. The next person they asked was Clara Barter, Maurice's mother, who did indeed help them out; Helen doesn't say, but this had to have had some effect on her early feelings about Maurice. She also remembers that she and her brothers and sisters had to walk to school on the Thoroughfare over the ice-covered rocks along the shore because the family who owned the farmhouse next door didn't want them walking by the house every day, as they would have had to do in order to get to the road. The lady of this house could be the Mrs. R. of the student minister's diary, and even though there is a twenty-year difference in time, the conclusions I reached earlier about her welcome of him may, at least, be complicated by this story of Helen's.

After several years, Mr. Smith was assigned to another lighthouse in the bay, and Helen and her mother and siblings went to live in the city near it. She returned to the Island as Maurice's wife.

In the summer she runs the post office which serves the Point.

The other place beside Rich's Cove which has had, until very recently, a year-round identity as a separate place is Head Harbor, at the southeastern end of the Island. It is the best harbor on the southern coast, protected from the wind and the sea by high land to the west and the east and by a ledge which runs part way across its entrance, on which the waves from the open sea beyond break spectacularly after a storm. It is this position on the seaward end of an outer island which made it most accessible to the best fishing in the days before gasoline engines, when such accessibility mattered.

It was also accessible to coastwise shipping; in the late nineteenth century lobster smacks all the way from New York would come in to Head Harbor to load, rather than to the town on the Thoroughfare at the other end of the Island. There was a thriving settlement with a store, and the people there had what seems to have been a complete independence from the town five miles away by the trail over the mountain. Now there is no winter population; Gooden Grant, who is ninety-six and the only indigenous inhabitant of Head Harbor, retired and moved to the Main in the winter when his wife died eleven years ago. He is living there with Archie Hutchinson, a lobsterman, and his wife, Eva, in their house and moves down with them every summer into his own house at Head Harbor. There are seven other houses, only four of which were inhabited during my first summer.

I got the feeling, not entirely substantiated, that if there ever was anything like a "rough section" on the Island, it was at Head Harbor. The place seems to have had a mild air of disrepute, not because of any feeling that the people from there were downright antisocial but that they were more independent than the rest of the already quite independent Island population—to the point of being what might be called ornery. There was what was known as a "lobster war" in the early fifties in this area of the Maine coast, in which invasions and counterinvasions of the territories of various communities produced a great deal of damage to fishing gear and even wharves, and during which there may have been some bloodshed; I've heard talk that Head Harbor, as distinct from the rest of the Island, was involved in these. I've also heard that at one point in the last fifty years there was a certain amount of feuding among the people down there. A summer person who was out hauling with one of the residents one bitter stormy day reported that he had refused to go back in, although the sea was making it harder and harder to haul his traps effectively, because his neighbor, with whom he was fighting at the time, was still out in his boat.

They were big men, given to broad action. Harold Turner remembers that Les Grant was exactly the length of a lobster trap lathe across the shoulders, as good a unit of measurement in those parts as any other; a lathe is thirty-six inches. Each spring, to continue a tradition started when Harold was a boy and Les a man, Harold would go down to Head Harbor, and he and Les would have a wrestle. In the ninety-second spring of his life Les said for the first time that he wasn't sure that he felt like wrestling that year, and he died a few months later. Les and his brother, Gooden, used to row fifty-five-gallon drums of kerosene the eleven miles from the Main to a landing place on the rocks of the eastern coast of the Island (so that they wouldn't have to row around Eastern Head and back into Head Harbor) and roll them the rest of the way, which was a half mile. Like his brother, Gooden was a big man when he was young—he weighed 205 pounds at the age of fourteen—but someone told me that he was not supposed to have been a good fighter, although tremendously strong, which says as much about which characteristics were worthy of attention down at Head Harbor as it does about Gooden's peaceful nature.

The history of Head Harbor is the history of Gooden Grant—because of his long life there, and also by default; in its heyday it was off by itself and thus generally excluded from whatever small amount of history was recorded in the town. What are left are the bits and pieces which lie scattered in the matrix of Gooden's memory—an old man's memory which retains single events and characters very clearly but the connections between them, like dates, only fuzzily.

The full realization of how old he is hit me most clearly one day when he referred to Canada as "the English Dominion"—not that it's so long since Canada attained its sovereignty but that the term conjures up such an ancient bias. Gooden's father, David M. Grant, who died in 1914 at the age of ninety, was born only nine years after the end of the War of 1812, and he grew up in Maine, where the proximity of a potentially hostile foreign power must have been felt strongly for a longer time than in most other parts of the country. Over the years a few hostile sparks have been struck from the contact between the fishermen of both countries, and there is still competition between the lobster fisheries. But, still, it takes a long past to connect Canada, even indirectly, with the Hanoverian tyrant across the Atlantic.

"I don't talk much about them old days now," Gooden says. "People will think I'm bragging." And, really, he doesn't; I felt a kind of modesty which

made him cannily resist being drawn out, supposedly an easy trick with very
old people. Out of the few visits we had with him the outlines of a good,
vigorous life emerged. As I make it out, after trying to fit the various scraps
of evidence in the notes of my conversations with him into some kind of a
whole, his father, David Grant, was born in interior Maine in a somewhat
urban environment and was college educated. When he was young—probably
in the 1840s—he came to the Island and paid fifteen dollars for a hundred-
acre farm down by the pond. He grazed five hundred sheep on the west side
of the pond, and Gooden says he never had to buy a pound of meat in his life.
He also fished and ran one of the stores in Head Harbor, of which Gooden says
there were three in 1900, patronized by the coasting lobster smacks as well
as by the local people. A measure of the bustle of the place at that time is the
fact that many of the supplies in David Grant's store came directly from
Boston—from the firm of Swallow and Fales, Wholesalers. Despite the activity,
there wasn't so much cash on the Island that there weren't some hard times.
People laid by the products of sea and land for the winter, but there were some
poor people around and Gooden remembers that before spring things got
tight. Fulfilling the traditional responsibility of community storekeeper, David
Grant would help them out. Gooden was born in 1876, when his father was
fifty-two. At the age of ten he began fishing from a rowboat, seining with hoop
nets for porgies and pressing them for their oil, which was used as the basis
of paint. It took one hundred porgies to make a gallon of oil, which he could
sell for one dollar. At fourteen he was lobstering alone from a peapod.

The place must have been lively. Gooden says that there were twenty
or thirty boys at Head Harbor in those days and that they used to go swimming
in the pond after a day's fishing. (The pond is about a half mile from the
harbor and hasn't changed much in eighty years; I swam in it daily, and I
thought it strange and wonderful, coming from Gooden's, that four generations
could be spanned by one living man's experience of the permanence and change
of one small place. How does the pond look to him now? Does he remember?
What does he remember?)

Gooden had his present house built in 1911, when he married a schoolteacher
from one of the big neighboring islands in the bay. When his father died in
1914, he closed the store but continued to sell gasoline as well as go fishing.
When Madeline died in 1961, he retired. Prominently on the wall, there is
a commendation from the Shell Oil Company in the form of a lettered gilt
plaque, which I guess Gooden is proud of but which looked shoddy next to the

deep grain of his life. I felt, naïvely, that they could have come up with a little better expression of the honor of having their product sold by such a man in such a place for so long.

Gooden had been sick the winter I was on the Island. When we came down to pay a call on him and Archie and Eva that spring, he was moving about outside one of the sheds, his back bent over at almost a right angle to his legs. ("Place gets messy when you're away.") He'd spent some time in the hospital and had great contempt for the experience ("Lots of them foreign doctors," with what I thought was a slightly nervous smile at his recognition of the fact that we ourselves might be more foreign than he imagined, "didn't see as they knew much"). He had felt pretty abandoned until a friend who was a doctor at the hospital came by, looked at him, went away and came back, saying he didn't see why Gooden was in there, telling him to get his coat and get out.

It reminded me of the story I'd heard of his brother Les. He had gone into the hospital with coronary difficulties and had undergone a series of tests, including an electrocardiogram, which, after electrodes had been attached to him and he had seen his heartbeat recorded on the strange machine, he described as having a total stranger "run that toilet paper through me." If that isn't a pretty clear description of an EKG, I don't know what is.

As I said, Gooden lives with Archie and Eva Hutchinson permanently, now that he is a widower, and during the summer they all live down at Gooden's house, and Archie hauls his traps out of Head Harbor. Archie is sixty-four, although Eva says he acts more like thirty. She generally says this in the middle of a party, as she watches Archie dancing cheek-to-cheek with someone, having put aside his accordion and allowed someone else to take over the provision of music. He works hard, but I guess I associate Archie mostly with parties, and I feel that to him summers on the Island mean feasting and dancing and drinking and making music as much as anything else. I heard that the family July 4th picnic was attended by eight children and twenty-three grandchildren and that it ended with most of the thirty-one throwing each other gleefully into the water. Eva works hard too, and she knows it; she had a hernia a couple of years ago—said she couldn't sit still unless she was watching *Gunsmoke* on TV, said her friends told her she'd pay for it later, and she did.

Julie and I went to a couple of parties at Archie's. They generally started out of a kind of spontaneous combustion—like the first one we went to, which seemed to have had its genesis when Jim Wilson, a college economist who has a house at Head Harbor, met Archie and his son Ray parked by the side of the road, taking a little refreshment. He joined them for a bit and then went home to dinner, near the end of which Archie and Ray stopped by to entertain the Wilsons with their squeeze boxes. It was generally agreed that a party might be a good idea, and Jim was dispatched to round up a few people while Archie and Ray went over to the house of Bob DeWitt for a short warmup session with Bob's sax. By the time we arrived, there was a good little dancing and drinking party going in the kitchen of Gooden's house, with music provided by Archie, sitting on the bed of the adjacent room. There were Jim and Sharon Wilson; Pat and Annie Haynes, the schoolteachers; Doug Archibald, a Cornell historian, and his wife, Mitzi; Ed Hodgins, a bachelor who lives on the mainland during the winter and moves into a little house next to Jim and Sharon in the summer. It was an occasion and directly stated as such ("If we don't have a good time tonight, it's our own fault," Archie kept saying), and this seemed awkward to me at first, but then I thought why does every gathering have to be the means to substantive communication, why can't a party be an end in itself? We were actively and purposefully having a party. Gooden sat with deep contentment in a chair placed in the doorway between the kitchen and the bedroom so that he could easily experience the music and the dancing, which was cramped, but not as much as in most of the night clubs I remember going to. I don't see how, but Archie got up at 5 A.M. that morning to go hauling.

Head Harbor—Gooden Grant's house

At a summer dance in town: Archie Hutchinson on accordion (flanked by Noyes MacDonald, retired fisherman, at the piano and Bob DeWitt, Episcopal bishop, on sax)

Gooden Grant

Rich's Cove—fish shacks

The Breezes' house in Rich's Cove, where we stayed in the summer

The oak tree, shown in the nineteenth-century photograph on page 105, has grown, the shed is gone, and there would have been too many people around in those days for a lady to have walked down to the rock in her nightgown.

Helen Barter

The lighthouse

Rich's Cove in winter

The Thoroughfare and the town, seen through winter vapor from the mailboat

The mailboat

Harold Turner running the mailboat
Harold van Doren and Irville Barter in the mailboat cabin

The view from the porch of Alice Hoskins' house, our winter home

Our winterized kitchen, exterior
Interior, with Julie

The frozen pond—Pat and Annie Haynes in the distance

Pat Tully and Bill Stevens in the iceboat

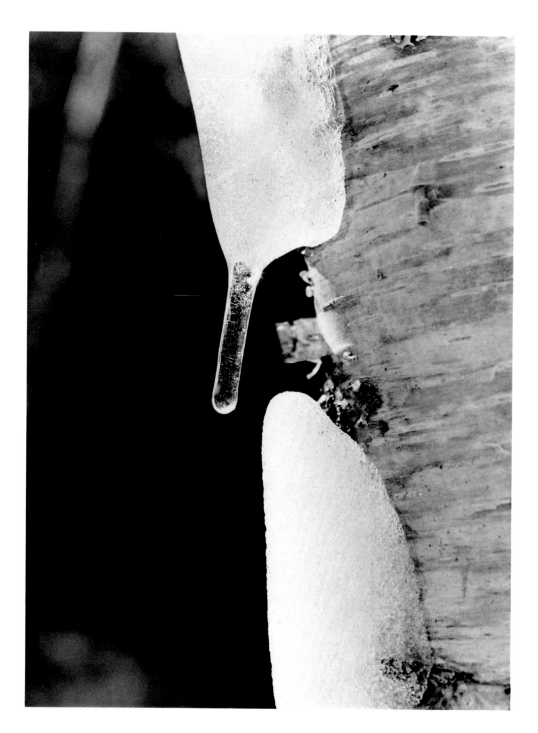

Icicle on a birch trunk

Winter woods, Moore's Harbor

Salt-water ice first forms in those coves where streams and runoffs have made the water fresher and, therefore, more susceptible to freezing. Successive tides push it up the beach.

The consistency of salt-water ice is soft but tough, like a strange kind of sherbet.
As the tide recedes, its mass is deposited on the irregularities of the shore.

The area of wetness left on the rocks by the ebbing tide freezes more
easily than the surrounding water.

A salt-water marsh—the tide has left a sheet of ice on a stream bank.

A couple of lobster boats, hauled up for the winter near the Thoroughfare, during a snowstorm

One of the fish shacks at Rich's Cove

The foredeck of Phil Alley's boat, seen through the windshield on a rough day

7

FISHING

The basic occupation of the Island is lobster fishing, as it has been the basic
occupation of the Maine coast for over a hundred years. The nineteenth-
century fishery was based on the canneries, which packed lobster meat and
sent it all over the world. At that time, lobsters were so plentiful that they could
be raked from under the seaweed at low tide or caught simply in baited hoop
nets. After the cannery-based fishery peaked in 1870 and was finally killed by
the establishment of a minimum length in 1895, there were still lobsters enough
to provide for a flourishing live market.

In 1910, which is about when the photograph on the following page was
probably made, the price of lobsters was four cents apiece, regardless of weight.
The fishery remained strong through the first half of this century. In 1940 there
was a boom; Skeet MacDonald, who lobsters from the Island from March
through November, recalls that in that year there was an extraordinarily good
annual catch, that the price held, and everybody decided to go lobstering. Then,
as I understand, a man could get 200 pounds from 60 to 75 traps hauled every
other day. It was hard work, because the traps were hauled from the bottom by
hand in many cases, but it was no harder than it is now, when one man hauling
alone with a special winch has to fish—every other day—200 traps to get 150
pounds. Those who have help—as Bill Barter does by fishing with his brother
Wayne—haul about 500 traps to make the operation pay off.

Lobsterman in pinkie, early in the century

At the end of the war, there was an enormous increase in the number of
lobstermen, as the returning veterans bought boats and gear with G.I. loans and
went hauling—many to drop out of full-time fishing when they found it was
harder than they had thought it would be. They made most of their living
other ways but kept their licenses and hauled part time, with the result that
now, according to the Maine Lobstermen's Association, an estimated 72 percent of holders of Maine lobster licenses fish only part of the time, and there
are fifteen hundred license holders in the Lewiston-Auburn area, which is
twenty miles inland. At present there is a scarcity of lobsters, the reasons for
and the solutions to which are many and various. I've heard it said that the
cooperation within the fishery necessary to deal with this scarcity is inhibited
by the presence of so many young fishermen who haven't made a commitment

to the fishery, being in the business only part time and figuring that if it doesn't work out they'll sell their gear and do something else.

The Island lobsterman sell to dealers on the Main, and it is the dealer who sells them their bait and some of their gear. There are a number of dealers in the area, and so there is a certain amount of competition among them for the individual lobsterman's supply, mostly in the form of a Christmas bonus, which is a small percentage of the individual's annual catch. Phil Alley bought a depth recorder with his bonus one year. The dealer has storage ability in the form of large pounds submerged in a quiet section of the harbor in which enormous quantities of lobsters can be held and fed until the passing of a seasonal abundance has raised the market price, and in this way they can cushion the results of rising and falling prices. Several years ago some lobstermen of the area which includes the Island formed a cooperative, in which the profits beyond a certain amount were redistributed among the members according to the volume of their catch sold to the co-op.

The price fluctuation is enormous. There is a seasonal scarcity and resulting rise in price in July, when the lobsters shed their old shells. They don't all shed at once, as each shedding lobster emits an enzyme which temporarily inhibits the shedding of others in the neighborhood, but there are always enough shedders around at this time to comprise a good percentage of the catch. Their meat is stringy and unpalatable, and the dealers pay much less for them, as they have to be kept in pounds until their shells harden and they can be sold at the regular price. On top of this, there was a general scarcity my first year on the Island, and the price—that is, the price paid to the lobstermen—went up astronomically to above $2 per pound from its norm of about $1.50. The dealers found that they just couldn't sell at that price, so by the end of July they had lowered their price to the wholesalers and had taken up the slack by lowering the price paid to the fishermen to $1.80, although the scarcity of lobster remained as severe as it had been with the higher price. By early August the price was down to $1.20 and threatening to go lower. The men in some of the ports were talking of a mass refusal to go out hauling or, if they did go out, a refusal to sell, even though an individual's ability to hold lobsters for a better price depends on the holding space available to him and his willingness to take the risk that a storm will break open the floating crates with the possible loss of a week's worth of lobsters.

It becomes evident that, on top of all the hard work, the lobsterman has to deal with a set of economic factors as tricky as if he were sitting around playing the stock market, particularly when you add to the instability of prices the constant threat that he may lose most or all of his gear in a storm. It's a strange combination of honest, backbreaking sweat and gambling.

I would never think of asking any of my fisherman friends on the Island what his annual income is, but I managed to get a well-founded opinion from off-island that the gross income range of a lobsterman, fishing four to five hundred traps full time for nine months, is eight to twelve thousand dollars a year. Half of that gross takes care of his expenses—bait, gear, gas and what he pays to the helper he must have to fish on that scale—leaving him with a net income range from lobstering of four to six thousand dollars a year. Depending on luck and skill, the fluctuation within and outside of this range is enormous, but four thousand dollars per year is still slightly below what the government calls the poverty level for a family of four; there's something wrong when a group of men who combine that much effort and skill with that much good old American initiative and daring to provide that much good food should be so slightly rewarded.

The future of the fishery is clouded. There have been other periods of shortage, and some think that periods of good and bad fishing come in cycles. Most are convinced that the lobster population is being diminished by over-fishing, and some even think that the point may be near when the population is so low that effective reproduction is impossible. State agencies, lobstermen associations and individual lobstermen (who as a type are about as indi-vidualistic as you can get) are pretty much agreed that some form of control is necessary, such as a limit to the number of traps or the limitation of licenses to those who fish a minimum number of traps, as a way of reserving the fishery to those who make their living from it.

Controls aimed at enhancing the breeding capacity are more difficult to arrive at, because amazingly little is known about the habits of lobsters, considering that men have been trying to outwit them for over a hundred years. As an example—fishermen have always assumed that lobsters migrate from shallow into deep water at some point in the fall. The individual lobster-man's guess as to when this point will take place in any one season is vital, for it will determine when he moves his traps out from shore, adding the necessary (and expensive) warp to take care of the extra depth. Last fall, Phil Alley moved some of his out at the traditional time but held some back inshore in the kind of experimentation which is typical of good fishermen, and he found that this had worked out—the inshore traps were still fishing better.

This is an annual guessing game based on a set of premises which most biologists now think are false. Most of them have come to the conclusion that lobsters don't move very much at all but are just more active in warmer water; in the winter the inshore water is cooled by the relatively cold land mass and stream runoff to a lower temperature than the deeper water, and in the summer the reverse is true. You'd think that this determination would have been confirmed to the point where, if true, it would be useful to the fishery, but what little is being discovered about lobster habits seems not to be passed on in any organized manner to the individual lobsterman. Furthermore, the individual fisherman is constantly experimenting in his own way by moving his strings of traps around according to feel. If he's been at it long enough, the chances are that this experimentation has resulted in a bunch of beliefs which have been proven empirically to him, if nobody else, and the whole business is too risky for him to depart radically from these.

In the meantime, what exactly does go on down there on the bottom as the lobster crawls around among the traps is still mainly a mystery, which can't be solved by observations of lobsters in captive conditions, or even by divers, whose presence would be disruptive.

Efficient dissemination of technical knowledge and agreement on conservation methods to protect the entire fishery are hampered by the traditionally high degree of competition in the lobster fishery. Over the years the fishing ports of Maine have established their several territories and defended them against all other lobstermen, and all of them have resisted any degree of control by the government, even though by now all observe the rules governing minimum size and the return of roe-bearing females. The degree of ethnocentricity is greater the further out to sea the port is; there is one island whose lobstermen all belong to the same family, for the simple reason that all others are prohibited by custom from fishing the area immediately around the island; these people deal with any new rules the government may devise with the assumption of the simple premise that, goddamnit, they were there before the State of Maine—which, indeed, their ancestors were. The lobstermen of another island, even further out, meet every year and decide on a closed season for the water immediately around them, which is a simple thing for them to do as nobody else dares to fish these waters.

The maintenance of territory has an enormous economic significance, as the out-island catches are consistently better. The methods of policing the various preserves are, of course, extralegal; the sea is open to all outside the three-mile limit and open to all Americans within that. (This, of course, is not much protection against international dragging operations just outside the three-mile limit, which are considered another large factor in the decrease of the Maine lobster population.) The usual system of sanctions which the defenders of territory use against interlopers progresses from tying a warning knot in the warp just below the buoy, through cutting off the last trap on a string, to, finally, cutting the warp just below the buoy, causing the loss of everything. The man who carries out this vigilante action takes a certain amount of care to hide his identity in order to prevent retaliation; however, these actions have sometimes escalated into "lobster wars," involving the destruction of lots of gear and the burning of docks, and there have been stories of gun battles, even though nobody talks about them much—at least to nosy types writing books.

As the need for some cooperation becomes more evident, and the ability to haul farther away from home grows, the territoriality is starting to break down. The lobstermen from the Island range into water which is also fished by boats out of the Main and boats from the large island ten miles away, but the shoal water immediately off the western coast and just outside the northern entrance to the Thoroughfare seem still exclusively theirs. The territory just off the eastern shore had been lost to the Island with the departure of most of the Riches, and boats from the Main come in close there. I tried to draw out Phil Alley, with whom I went hauling, on the question of territory, but I couldn't entice other than charitable opinions of the Main lobstermen out of him—except for once, when someone had set a string of traps out in the middle of the bay so close to those of his which were already there that the two strings could have easily fouled each other, and even then all he said was "Wonder why they do that?" and "Don't do no good to speak to them." It seems impossible that he or any other of my friends on the Island would do violence to off-island traps set too close to their shores, but I wouldn't be too sure.

The trap which is most used now on the Maine coast is a semi-round crate of wood three feet long and a foot and a half high, divided into two compartments and having a lid, hinged by leather straps, which is opened for emptying and baiting. The lobster enters through one of two meshed funnels in the opposite sides of the baited compartment, is unable to find its way out and is generally led through the wide end of a third funnel into another compartment of the trap. It is imprisoned by the narrow end of this last funnel as well as the other two at right angles to it. The last compartment is called the parlor, and, although some people refer to the baited first half of the trap as the "fishing end," Phil and others call it the "kitchen," which gives the cozy image of the lobster as someone coming to call, entering the house through the kitchen (as one does in most Maine houses) and then taking his ease in the parlor.

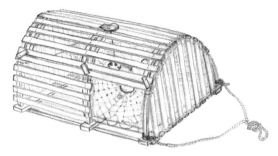

Line, called potwarp (or just warp), of a length appropriate to the depth being fished, runs from one end of the trap to another trap (in the case of a string of two traps) and then up to the buoy on the surface. Interspersed along the warp are a number of toggles, which serve to keep the slack from gathering on the bottom at low tide and getting tangled or fouling a ledge. Instead, the extra warp lies on or near the surface, ready to foul the propellers of the boats of summer people who don't know to steer clear of it—which, under the gaze of eternity, seems the preferable alternative. (Never go between a lobster buoy and its toggle or, better still, always go downwind or down-current of the buoy, unless you're in York Narrows, where there are so many that going downwind of one buoy will put you upwind and in position to foul another.)

The standard lobster boat is thirty-four feet long with a wide beam and a draft of about three feet. The foredeck, under which the engine and not much else is housed, extends about half the length of the boat; just aft of it, a wheelhouse with no back to it partially shelters the man at the helm and, at the most, two or three others crowded in alongside him. There is a large after space to hold bait barrels and to allow two people to work freely and a raised afterdeck large enough to hold a pile of traps stacked along it. The gunwales on each side are just wide enough to hold the traps lengthwise after they have been hauled for emptying and cleaning, and are called washboards. The long foredecks seem to split a head-on sea like a knife, and to me they are the most beautiful boats in the world.

A day of lobstering is long and hard—much more so than I had ever realized all those previous summers when, traveling about the coastal waters, I would wave at working lobstermen and be slightly hurt when they didn't have the time or a spare hand to wave back. Two men hauling together can tend as many as five hundred traps, but Phil Alley, with whom I went out during my first year on the Island, hauls alone, which means that in a twelve-hour day he can tend about 150 traps. He also has a herring weir at Moore's Harbor with Gordon Chapin and his son Carol, so in order to get the little rest he does get, he hauls every other day. He says there are a lot of men—younger men—who work harder, but I can't quite see how. Each man seems to have his own schedule; some haul half of their traps one day and the other half the next, and some tend all of them every other day; in either case the trap is down on the bottom attracting lobsters for at least a day. Of course, these patterns are constantly being interrupted by bad weather, which can keep a boat in harbor for a week or more.

Phil gets out to his boat about six in the morning, warms up the motor, gets into his yellow apron, takes the lid off the bait barrel (thereby enriching the morning air), rolls out a strip of red carpet he lays along the working area of the starboard rail for firm footing and casts off. In general terms, the day's work involves finding each of his strings of traps scattered within the territory of the Island, hauling them, emptying and rebaiting each trap and returning each string to the water. The first step is to find the buoy, the surface of which is painted in his special colors and has his license number carved on it. In the fog, this is well-nigh impossible, so nobody goes out in a thick-of-fog; in a chop, locating the buoys is at best difficult, as they are intermittently hidden and momentarily revealed in the troughs and crests of the sea. The job is to keep track of a number of buoys which are scattered about the bay and which he is constantly moving from one spot to another to see if they'll fish any better. Phil accomplishes this by taking bearings on islands and ledges, when he sets a string in a new location, and making a few notes on the wood of a small box in front of him which holds the pegs used to hold shut the lobsters' claws. Still, there would be a few times in every day when he couldn't lay his eye on a buoy he was sure he'd find in a certain spot (". . . Thought I had another pair here") or, after going around in several circles within one group of his buoys, he would forget which strings he'd already hauled ("Now you *know* that's funny—I can't remember hauling that one"). He never uses a chart; I suppose there was one somewhere on the boat, but after fishing the area for so many years, he doesn't have to.

During the warmer weather, as I've said, the best fishing is in shallow water, and it is usually right off a ledge which can be showing at low tide with an angry sea breaking on it. Working in as close as ten feet to one of these ledges to pick up the buoy of a string of traps is tricky, particularly if all the work of boat handling and hauling has to be done by one man. The greatest danger in this particular part of the procedure is that the propeller will get tangled in the line from his own or another string of traps, and the immobilized boat will be picked up by a swell and carried crashing onto the rock. Jack MacDonald once indicated the strength of one of these swells which break on a ledge by describing to me what it felt like, when he was being carried in on one from a good way off shore, to open up a powerful marine engine and realize that he was *just barely* going faster than the force under his boat. ("You want to watch out for them.")

After years of carefully coming up to buoys, docks, other boats and so on from downwind, I was interested to find out that Phil, I suppose like every other lobsterman, can pick up a buoy coming at it from any direction—as, of course, he has to, because downwind of a certain number of buoys at certain tides may be nothing but bare ledge. Leaning over the side and gaffing the warp starts a series of actions which are so familiar as to be second nature to him but which are performed in infinitely varying conditions. At some point, and for many different reasons, a lobsterman decides what side of the boat he's going to fish from, and this choice determines the entire layout of the boat, including the position of the wheel. Phil steered and picked up from the starboard side, which meant that the traps ended up on the starboard rail, but many fishermen end up doing it all from the port side, although, having been out only with Phil, I can't imagine how. It seems to have nothing to do with right- or left-handedness, but it is still so deeply ingrained that, if a man buys a boat which is rigged to be worked from the wrong side, he will have to have it changed around at a good deal of expense.

With an easy movement, Phil throws the line over the block on a davit which swings out from the boat and into the groove of the pot hauler, which he has started, and which starts the traps up from the bottom, unless one of them is hung up on a ledge. In that case he will move around the location of the hung trap, trying to free it by positioning the boat so that the pull is from a series of different angles, while the braking system of the pot hauler maintains a constant pressure on the line. At these times I noticed that Phil drew away from the straining line around the pot hauler and the block, and the reason for this extreme caution hit me: there is a certain amount of elasticity in the potwarp when it is under this enormous strain, and if it should part, or if the

124   trap won't come free and the line has to be pulled out of the groove of the pot hauler under this strain and happens to catch a hand or an arm, a man will be pulled over the side, to be held under by the tension of the line from the caught trap. When a foot is caught in the warp which is going out after the traps have been pushed overboard and are rapidly sinking, and a man is carried overboard tangled in it, there is at least some chance that he can be hauled up by his partner, as he is only being held down by the weight of the traps, but if the trap is fouled on the bottom, his only chance is to cut himself loose. I have never seen a lobsterman wearing a sheath knife. This is like the common inability to swim among Maine fishermen; the water is so cold and you are so fully dressed that you can't stay alive in it for long enough to make much of a difference, and so the trick is to stay aboard. It doesn't always work, however; I heard once of a man dragged overboard by the warp from an outgoing trap while hauling with a partner, who panicked so badly that he broke off the handle of the throttle and had to watch helplessly from the immobilized boat as the young man drowned. Every lobsterman is aware of similar disaster, and Phil handles the straining warp with care and lets the slack run out overboard as it comes off the wheel of the pot hauler rather than allowing it to collect inside the boat, where it could catch an ankle as it goes out later. Also, it was clear that he knew enough to quit at the point at which the trouble and danger involved in freeing a hung trap outweighed the chance of its loss (ten dollars per trap, not including line), in the hope that the tide would free it by the next time he hauled, which it generally did.

When each trap breaks the surface of the water, it is hauled onto the washboard. It was at this point once that Phil came the closest he's ever come to going overboard; just at the point of his farthest reach over the side to grab a trap, a sudden steep wave hit the port side, careening the boat over. The way he remembers how close it was is that his feet left the deck. Hauling alone, the lobsterman has nobody to turn the boat, although the natural tendency would be for it to fall off the direction of the sea and wind and go into a circle—after a time. But even assuming that the empty boat would pass nearby, there would still be the problem of grabbing hold and hauling yourself over the high sides. Considering this in a period of gloominess, some fishermen let a line trail astern to grab on to. Phil certainly didn't dwell on the dangers, and he didn't even talk about them except in response to my questions, but I found that they were in the front of my own mind as we lurched about on these waters which were so much stronger—not even to mention so much colder—than I was accustomed to.

The two traps of the string (there are some single-trap strings), lying alongside one another on the washboard, are now opened and the contents removed. The short lobsters—those whose body shells measure less than three and three-sixteenths inches according to Phil's eye or, in case of doubt, by a special gauge which everyone carries—are thrown overboard, and the keepers are put aside. At that time four keepers in one trap wasn't bad; Maurice Barter can remember getting fifteen in a trap one haul about ten years ago, which is his personal record. The trap is fresh-baited by spearing, with a special eyed spike, either a twine bag full of salt herring or a salted redfish from a large barrel, threading a piece of twine tied into the trap through the eye and drawing the spike and twine out through the bag or the redfish, closing the door of the trap and lashing the bait-laden twine onto a cleat outside. All of this time the boat has been in a combination of helm position and throttle to keep it off that ledge which is breaking angrily fifteen yards away, and to hold the stern— that is, the propeller—away from fouling the buoy line trailing aft. After the cleaning and baiting operation has been completed in as little time as possible, Phil will decide on whether he wants to set the string in approximately the same spot or move it to another. I've seen him, when he wanted to move it, gun the boat ahead full throttle for a half mile while holding on to fifty feet of line, a toggle and a buoy, churning up the water behind him. He's a big man. At the right spot the traps are pushed off the washboard in such a way that they'll land right side up on the bottom, the warp is let go, and the string is set.

While he charges ahead to the next string, or where he thinks the next string out to be, holding the helm with his body, he takes up the kept lobsters and, holding them down in front of him, pushes a small peg of wood into the joint of each crusher claw to keep them from destroying each other. He calls this putting on the handcuffs. When the lobster bites—and even Phil gets bitten a lot some days—the trick is to stay still, because if you do what comes naturally and pull your hand away, the flesh can get ripped open. As it is, after the bites and piercings from the "thorns," which lie between the claws and the body, have been bathed in salt water all day, your hands can hurt in the evening.

The pattern of movements which I've described is repeated, in Phil's case, about 150 times in the day, until he has tended all his traps. The tending of this number of traps in one working day requires a pace which is more like a rush than a steady push. Phil is in constant motion; there is not even rest between strings, as he opens up to full throttle to reach the next buoy in the shortest possible time. The first day I went out with him, we cast off at six-thirty, and he didn't take a break until ten-thirty. This means that there was *total* concentration as well as uninterrupted movement for four hours.

Then, after shoving the last trap of one string off the washboard, instead of going full throttle for the next buoy he slowed down to about half throttle and opened up a thermos of tea and ate a couple of cookies. He didn't sit down, and as a matter of fact there is nowhere to sit on the boat—no high stool usually used by helmsmen. That break took all of three minutes, and there was another one later on, but those were all. Another, more relaxed, day we tied up to a friendly buoy in Duck Harbor for a leisurely half-hour lunch, sitting on the washboard. It was a measure of how far I'd come along that, sitting next to the salt-herring bait barrel, I was able to eat a can of sardines and that I was able to ignore (almost) the yellow jackets which were attracted to the oil of the bait. Phil remembered that when he and the Chapins were salting down herring at Moore's Harbor they would have twenty-five or thirty yellow jackets on each arm, drawn by the oil, and they would not be stung.

Phil doesn't carry a watch, in somewhat the same way that he doesn't look at a chart. He really doesn't need one, as he continues pushing forward from one string to the other until he's through, unable to go any faster simply because he is always working at top speed. Of course, like all fishermen, he has an interior clock based on the tide, and the degree to which the tide current is setting down through a certain passage or the amount of rock showing on a certain ledge will show him that it's about noon and time to call Edna on the radio (". . . blowed up a bit coming back to the Thoroughfare . . . got most of 'em out here in the bay . . . ayeh . . . O.K. . . . KMA 3984 Mobile . . . out"). I asked if Edna ever came out with him, and he said no, she was a farm girl, didn't like it much. (Just in the past few years, I have heard of a few of the young wives going hauling with their husbands.)

Phil generally gets in a little after 4 P.M.—nearly ten hours of steady work, with perhaps two short breaks, after starting out in the morning. After that he has about an hour of work—perhaps placing the lobsters in storage crates anchored alongside the boat's mooring if he wants to hold them for a while because of a price drop, and always flushing and scrubbing down the boat. It's this care which makes Phil's boat seem a little more elegant—which is to say less smelly—to uninitiated types like me than a lot of lobster boats. By five in the afternoon he is home and having dinner. After a day of hauling, he says, he's likely to be fidgety for quite a time, as he winds down from the frantic pace of the day. I don't imagine there's much chance for him to get too fidgety, however, as most nights in the summer and fall he's tending the herring weir which he and the Chapins operate down at Moore's Harbor.

Virginia MacDonald, after forty years of living with a lobsterman, says that she has resigned herself to the conclusion that fishermen like Skeet and Phil don't go out of business until they die. They start out young as well. When Gordon and Maybel Chapin's son was ten years old, he used to play in an old skiff which had found its way to beneath an apple tree near their house. When it rained, he used to say that the boat was leaking and bail. One of the ever-present Island "uncles" had made him a couple of small traps, which he used to play at setting, and one night his father slipped a lobster from the previous day's catch into one of these. In the morning the little boy was excited but immediately noticed that the lobster's claw was pegged. This last summer Jack MacDonald's eleven-year-old son, Danny, started lobstering. Jack got him a license as his helper, which he is on occasion, and all July and August he hauled three traps set out in the Thoroughfare from a skiff with a ten-horse outboard. He wore a life preserver, and his father casually watched him like a hawk, but he was by himself. He'd started.

SCALLOPING

The only fisherman left on the Island that winter after November and the end of lobstering for the year was Jack MacDonald, and he went scalloping. Harold van Doren, who had been helping him haul lobsters earlier as a supplement to his garage business, went with him. The conversion of a lobster boat to a scallop dragger is difficult and expensive for someone on the Main, but down on the Island, away from welding shops, the supply of materials and tools and the like, it was a job to test a man's ingenuity, talent and willingness to pay the price of living and working on the Island. Jack had all of these. He was born on the mainland thirty-six years ago and raised there; he moved to the Island with his wife, Belvia, fifteen years ago. They have two kids in the school—Danny, who is eleven, and Juanita, nine. Jack had two uncles and a sister on the Island already, and he established himself and his family here with their help and by his own energy and talent. As the only full-time, year-round fisherman, living entirely off his income from fishing, he's something of a keystone in the economic structure of the Island. His new house is a good omen for the future.

Jack had been scalloping from time to time for fifteen years—"just for a mess"

—using comparatively light rope drags and a "gin pole" to hoist the drags high enough above the deck to allow them to be emptied, and he had been able to convert his boat from lobstering to scalloping in ten minutes. Now he would be hauling two steel drags, each weighing 150 pounds, over the bottom of the bay and having to raise them and their loads of rock, kelp, scallops and God knows what from the bottom to about four feet in the air above the gunwale—a combined weight of half a ton on some hauls. Just dragging this recalcitrant weight around on the bottom and hauling it to the surface is hard on a lobster boat (which, when powered by a marine engine, is about the sturdiest boat around for its size), but the effort of lifting the laden drags in the air, their weight now being dead weight, unassisted by water, is a killer. Jack notices that the boat has to be pumped out a lot more often now than when it was used solely for lobstering.

A mast with a boom, capable of supporting all this weight, must be stepped into the wooden hull. The pot hauler which used to haul lobster traps must be replaced by a winch holding six hundred feet of wire cable three-eighths inch thick. Plywood sheathing is put along the side of the boat to take some of the punishment of the drags, and a long dump box is secured to one of the gunwales, into which the load of the drags can be emptied for sorting.

There was something about the addition of all of this heavy metal and machinery to a wooden boat set afloat on the wintry seas that seemed to me, a layman, mad. I got the idea that Jack himself was pretty respectful of what he was requiring of the boat. It took him and Harold about two months to make the conversion, what with testing, finding problems and solving them, and they didn't start dragging until February. I had asked to go out, but Jack wasn't sure enough of the gear to take the time to watch out for a superfluous photographer; I'd guess that if something gave, a few pretty dramatic things might have happened.

Each of the two drags is about three feet square. The side which drags over the bottom is made of heavy steel mesh—actually a series of rings joined by links—and the other side is nylon mesh. These two surfaces are held open by a steel frame to form a mouth into which the scallops are drawn as the whole contraption jolts over the bottom. At the other end, the chain side and the nylon side end in two lengths of wood, which are bolted shut during the drag but which can be opened when the drags are hoisted up to spill the catch into the dump tray. There are two of these, mounted alongside each other on a yoke. The basic design is the same as Jack has always remembered it; fishermen are conservative, and tools tend to stay the same until some innovative type among them tries something new, the laughter dies down, the curiosity cautiously begins and the new tool or technique is adopted.

As presently designed, the drag is only about ten percent efficient. The scallops lie on the bottom and, sensing the approaching drag, propel themselves out of the way by opening and closing their shells, drawing the water in at the open end and expelling it at the hinged end. They can go like hell, some jumping over the top of the mouth and some to the side, and about ninety percent escape. The efficiency of the drag could be increased by enlarging the mouth, but, perhaps because it would make handling more awkward, this hasn't been done yet. It's probably a good thing; with a more efficient method the scallop population would be depleted even faster than it is now.

All scallop drags are built from scratch, and it seemed that most of them in the area, including Jack's, were being made by Lump Cousins and his son John at their garage on the Main. The only times I remember seeing Lump sit down was when he was at his camp on the pond of the Island or when he was driving me from the airport to the Main; he's one of those people who are in constant movement. Just as soon as the rush of the summer's auto work was over, the garage began to fill up with his fisherman customers. There seems to be a general rule on the coast of Maine that you never just contract for a job of work and then walk away to return in expectation of its being finished. This general rule is sometimes broken in the case of summer people, who are notoriously impatient, but the State-of-Mainer tends to hang around as much as he can, occasionally lending a hand to the expert but mainly just shooting the breeze and pushing the work along by his, the client's, presence. Lump and John didn't need to be pushed along, but it's a community habit, and the garage seemed to me to have the feel of the kind of gathering place which is usually associated with an old country store. The difference was that, instead of the wise, lovable old storekeeper leaning on the counter watching the checkers game, there would be Lump tearing around among his customers, doing a bit of welding here, throwing himself under a car there and generally keeping about six jobs going at the same time in what seemed to be a contented frenzy.

I didn't get out with Jack and Harold until the end of March, right before the end of the scalloping season. The temperature was in the twenties—luxurious warmth compared to many of the days they'd been out that winter—and it threatened snow. In winter it's absolutely essential to close in the wheelhouse, which is normally open on the after side for easy access to the gear, and most fishermen accomplish this with a plywood partition and a door, but Jack had gotten behind and was using canvas to complete his shelter. The basic heating device for the cabin of a lobster boat is the exhaust pipe, which runs from the engine through the cabin and out through the roof. As those of us who have accidentally touched it know, it gives off a lot of heat. If you stay inside you can keep warm, but if you have to be in and out, as you do scalloping, you stay cold most of the day. At least I did, and I was bundled up.

The dragging operation starts with the bulk of the two drags on their yoke being raised above the level of the gunwales by the winch, operated by Jack, swung over the side by Harold and then lowered. It's vital that the drags end right side up on the bottom, because if the nylon twine is dragged over the rocks it will inevitably tear.

Scallop beds are small and scattered; they are generally gravel or cobble-stones, surrounded by ledge or mud, and they generally extend less than a quarter mile in any direction. To fish these beds a man has to know them as well as a farmer knows his fields after a lifetime of looking and walking on them, which is a familiarity hard to come by if you're floating anywhere from twenty to fifty feet above them with an occasional ledge as a visible landmark. The consequences of a mistake—aside from not getting any scallops—are impressive; the bed is dragged as close to the edge as possible, and going over the edge can easily result in the drags' being capsized on a ledge and torn.

The basic tool used to find and drag the beds is the fathometer, which, to put it simply, bounces an electrical impulse off the bottom and measures the distance traveled. The returning echo not only shows the distance to the bottom but also, by the strength or weakness of the indicator light, the bottom's character; mud, for example, presents a yielding, and therefore weaker, bouncing surface than ledge.

The fathometer is a big help, but the knowledge of the bottom basically comes from the multitude of scattered pieces of information which Jack, like all fishermen, is constantly ingesting and storing. The fathometer lets you know your nearly exact position by a comparison of the depth shown on it with the depth marked on a chart, or it serves to warn you of the ledge you're about to hit when you're running a course in the fog. Given the minimum visibility required for hauling traps or scalloping, the more reliable method is to accumulate an encyclopedia of bearings for your local area, so you can line up two points of land to give yourself a course which can be run until you reach a certain bearing-obtained point, or to give yourself a course which can be combined with a compass course. The bearing points, of course, have to show above high tide, because the look of a certain stretch of water is totally different at different tides. The degree to which the landmarks show is also important. Thus, for example, in negotiating the jungle of rocks around Nathan's Island on your way to the Island: if the tide is high enough so that the rock which looks like a lopsided turtle is covered beyond where the neck would stick out if it were a real turtle, you can run SSE until you bring Rita Parker and Katherine Butler's house out from behind the easternmost ledge showing at that particular tide, at which point you can turn in toward the Thoroughfare; or, negotiating an even narrower passage around Nathan's, you put the church steeple right over a bunch of trees on the eastern end of Flake Island (that is, you line them up) and then go through. As the bearing points rot away or get painted, the data change ("Buy Maine Coast property and become a bearing point"). Anyway, in twenty years of fishing Jack had stored up quite a few of these pieces of evidence.

However, when you're scalloping, that's just the beginning of it. As I've said, the small margin for error requires an intimacy with the bottom on the scale of feet, not yards. As the quarter ton of drag lurched over this unseen but tenderly felt terrain, a strange analogy occurred to me. At first, all I felt was the crushing force being used to get all that steel moving like a great bulldozer over the virgin territory of complicated marine life, which I imagined the bottom to be, tearing up everything in its way. Then, I suddenly realized that Jack was *feeling* the bottom, physically, with great delicacy—a delicacy which became apparent when I reduced all that weight and horsepower and accompanying noise to the scale of a man sitting in a drifting canoe pulling a small lead weight on the end of a string across a gravel bottom and feeling every little bump and resistance. It was simply a different scale. Jack was at the helm with his hand on the throttle and his eyes on the fathometer, causing what sounded and felt, through the lurches of the boat, like complete havoc, but his real hand was the boat itself and the engine his muscle. His concentration was complete; I once asked him a question in the middle of the operation; he interrupted his concentration out of friendliness and courtesy, and the drag hit a ledge. All of this maneuvering must be done while maintaining the boat at a slight angle, with the stern away from the line of pull in order to keep the cable out of the propeller. One doesn't feel right about waxing poetic in such circumstances, so all I could think of to say was that he must know the bottom pretty well; he replied that it helps some.

Thinking later about the noise, I realized that modern fishermen feel as strong a personal connection with their motors as they are supposed by tradition to feel about their boats. It's the motor which develops its own particular set of idiosyncrasies and is very personally cursed. In an earlier age, when sail power moved boats along at a slower pace, it was the hull which could be felt personally, with every creak and pitch being familiar to the owner. Now, the hull is not much more than the container for the motor.

For most of my adult life I've been a trout fisherman, and I've always thought that the subtlest, most delicate fishing in the world was laying a dry fly gently down on the surface of a pool. Now I don't know—maybe it's dragging a quarter ton of metal over the bottom of the bay.

The length of the drag depends on Jack's sense of when the drags are full or when they foul on a ledge. How he can tell the difference between four hundred and five hundred pounds being yanked reluctantly over the bottom I can't imagine, but, again, it's a matter of scale and sensitivity. If the drag gets hung up, he releases it by moving the boat so that the angle of pull is different, a method I remember using often to free a four-ounce trolling lure snagged on the bottom of a pond. The winch is put into gear, and the drags are hauled to the surface and drawn along with the boat for a while to flush them of some of the gravel and then raised by the boom to above the dump box, where the bolts holding the two-by-fours together to form the bottom of the drag are pulled and the contents of the drags dumped. Hopefully, the contents fall into the dump box; if a swell comes along at the wrong moment, and the drags swing enough, the whole lot can go overboard.

It's in this part of the operation that most of the special danger of scalloping occurs. The winches in some boats are hydraulic, but most have geared winches, the cogwheels of which are open; it's pretty easy to lose your balance in a pitching boat, and the turning teeth are very receptive to a loose sleeve or the like. By the time I went out, two scallop fishermen on the Main had already that season lost fingers to the winches. In the slightest sea, the laden drags, as they swing above the dump tray, can knock a man overboard into water which will likely freeze him to death in a minute, even if he manages to stay afloat in all the clothing he has to wear. When there's much of a sea running, most scallopers will quit for the day, unless they can find a bed to drag in the lee of a ledge, and the day I went with Jack and Harold they stopped dragging at midday for that reason. As it was, it was all I could do to handle one of the pair of drags.

The empty drags are lowered in the same or a new bed for the next drag, unless one of the rings or links needs to be repaired. Repairs are done on a pitching deck with a spare rock used as an anvil; Harold has to choose between clumsy gloves and cold fingers, and, being a mechanic, he tends to choose the latter. During the drag he sorts out the scallops from the miscellany of the bottom and throws them into a small crate. The miscellany was mostly rocks, kelp and sea colander with an occasional sea cucumber or starfish, and at times I wondered what was left down there as a marine environment. Occasionally surprises come up in the drags—parts of boats, old bottles, pieces of eight. The dump box is emptied by removing its outside wall and pushing the residue overboard.

Harold turns to shelling for the rest of the drag, although very often he can't get them all done before it's time to haul up the drags again, and some shelling has to be left for later. In a spare, quick set of movements which it takes a year to learn properly, the scallops are opened with a knife and the rim (guts) thrown overboard. What is kept is the muscle which opens and closes the shell, and this is thrown into a mesh-sided wash basket for later rinsing in the sea. There is a square opening in the side of the wheelhouse partition for the shelling operation, but Harold likes to shell outside when the sea and weather permit. The gulls go crazier over scallop guts—diving closer to the boat—than I'd even seen them act over lobster bait. Jack told me that they won't feed alongside a boat which is standing still, as it's difficult for them to take off when close in the lee of anything. There is talk of the development of a process for turning the rim into poultry feed, so the gulls may be deprived soon.

The scallops (now in their familiar form) are thrown into the wash basket, rinsed and put into a five-gallon garbage car; it seems strange that the produce of all that time and muscle should fit into such a small space. I had gloomy thoughts of the garbage can falling overboard, when it was unloaded at the dealer's dock on the Main or when Harold carried it up to be weighed. Actually, just how full it is is something of a secret; a good day's catch is 100 to 150 pounds (the price that day was $1.50 per pound), and the difference between a half-full garbage can and a three-quarter-full one can be measured in a fair amount of money. Fishing is basically a competition for a limited resource, which is getting more limited each year, despite cycles of relative plenty and scarcity. There is no way that a lobsterman can hide the location of his traps—his distinctively marked buoys are there floating on the surface for everyone to see— but in scalloping it is possible to confuse the competition, and, in a more or less amiable way, everyone is out trying to do just that. One day the next summer I was hauling lobster traps with Phil Alley, and we were listening to the dialogue on the radio—one boat asking another how it was doing, and the reply coming back that it wasn't fishing too good over here, or: "Making any money?" to which "Oh, a little" might as easily as not have indicated an enormous haul. Phil remarked that, if you listened to the radio enough, you'd *never* go out, be scared half to death.

Pulling away from the dealer's dock on the Main and heading back to the Island, Jack and Harold relaxed for the first time in five hours, which was only half of the day they would have spent dragging if the seas had remained calm. It started to snow lightly. Jack opened his lunch and called Belvia on the radio. That night I ate fresh scallops, which in the flush of bachelor cookery I ruined by adding too much vermouth.

Bill Barter plans to go scalloping this winter with his brother Wayne. Jack and Harold will go again, and the Island moves on.

WEIR

Phil Alley and the Chapins operate their herring weir in Moore's Harbor during the spring, summer and fall. A weir is essentially a trap set in the middle of a cove, into which the herring school will be drawn as a result of its nightly forays inshore in search of food. As a trapping operation, weir tending is completely different in technique and basic nature from every other kind of fishing, including lobstering. The weir sits in one place, and, although it is a trap like a lobster trap, it cannot be moved, and the fish in the course of their mysterious migrations have to find their way to it, rather than its being moved to where they are likely to be.

Simply because it can't be moved, building and maintaining a weir is an enormous gamble. Phil and the Chapins built theirs in 1940, when nobody was going after herring in a big way, and the Maine sardine industry, which is heavily publicized now, was nonexistent. Herring were used for lobster bait, rather than being cooked and packed into cans for human food. The thought behind their building of the weir was that if the small fish, called "brit," were around each year, and the purse seiners were getting the big herring outside, the medium or sardine-size herring must be around somewhere, and Moore's Harbor looked like it might be a likely place for them to come inshore.

Strictly by hindsight, I can see why this would be so; the mouth of the harbor faces southwest into the teeth of the weather, the currents are strong enough to keep it ice-free in the worst winters and, looking out, you can easily see it as a gaping mouth ready to receive all kinds of things from the open sea. So it did, and although the catch dropped off in the late fifties and early sixties, the herring began coming back into the coves along the coast about five years ago— and so many came into the weir at Moore's Harbor that it became famous in the area. One expert is quoted as saying that Phil has "one of those places—if there are any fish he'll get his share." In the Maine manner of speaking "his share" means a lot. It could have turned out otherwise over the years, and that it didn't is the result of a kind of deep trapper's intuition and patience.

The heart of the weir is the pound, a circular enclosure about fifty feet in diameter, in which the captured herring are held. It is made out of netting, called twine, permanently secured to forty-five-foot spruce pilings driven into the bottom. There is a gate on the inside of the pound, and leads of twine permanently secured to pilings extend out—on one side to the northern shore of the cove which makes up the end of Moore's Harbor and on the other side about halfway to a point of land at the end of the southern shore of this cove. When Phil and the Chapins built the weir, they made the pound and the leads out of brush, secured to rails which run between the pilings, but when twine became cheaper, they switched to a combination of twine and a layer of brush as protection from the force of the waves. After each winter most of the brush has to be replaced, and some of the pilings have to be driven into the mud again.

From the middle of April to about the end of May the pile-driving float, which I'd seen all winter sitting high and dry on the shore, was moored out by the weir, piled high with new brush, when it wasn't being used for driving. Someone told me they once saw Phil wrap his arms around one of the huge pilings and lift it up out of the mud, but it takes a machine to drive one back in. This consists of a small motor secured to the float and used to haul the two-hundred-pound driving head to the top of a twenty-foot tower so that it can be dropped onto the top of the piling. The technique is to position the pile driver on its float directly over the piling to be driven, holding the piling steady, while someone takes a couple of turns with the hauling line around the spinning drum of the motor, tightens up and raises the head to the top of the tower and then releases it at exactly the right moment by flipping the three turns of line off the end of the drum. The consequence of not getting the line off the drum in time is that the head will go through the top of the tower, and the consequence of getting caught in the slack of the line as it's released from the drum is to be hauled into the air by two hundred pounds of falling steel—like getting a foot caught in the warp of a lobster trap going overboard, but being dragged up, not down. There is a grace to the operation, performed on a floating raft, and a degree of collaboration between the mind and muscle of a skilled man and the functioning of a basic machine which is very impressive.

When the herring come in, they come in at dusk through the wide opening between the end of the northern lead and the shore and up into head of the cove, searching after the tiny shrimplike animals and diatoms on which they feed. The time of day, not the tide, is the important factor in this movement. Every evening—in the summers about eight o'clock—Phil, Carol and Gordon come down and go out into the area between the leads to see if they have come in. On moonlit nights the herring used to be detected by a "feeling stick," which was simply a stick passed through the water upright so that it would come into contact with the mass of swimming bodies. On dark nights, when there is phosphorescence, a tap of the heel on the bottom of the skiff will send the herring scattering to reveal their presence by the "fire" they stir up. Nowadays, the standard detection device is a small battery-powered fathometer, carried in the small boat to bounce a weak but discernible signal off the solidity of the herring school. If the fish are in the cove all the way, the twine from the ends of both leads is set to both shores, and they are corralled. If there are no fish being held in it from a previous run, the gates to the pound are opened; at first light the school starts to move out to sea and are led into the enclosure, where they swim perpetually in a circle, always missing the gate. If there are already fish being held in the pound from an earlier run, the gates are kept closed and are opened just before first light.

When Phil and the Chapins consider that there is a sufficient quantity in the pound, the dealer on the Main is called and the sixty-foot-long carrier comes down to pump the herring out of the pound into its hold. A large net is passed under the fish, who in their desperation stay near the surface. One end of the net is secured to the factory carrier lying just outside the wall of the pound, and the other end is drawn into a dory by Phil, Carol and Gordon, condensing the fish into an ever-decreasing pocket. A large vacuum hose is stuck into the center of this pocket, and the herring are pumped up it into the hold and taken off to the cannery.

The times which Julie and I—or sometimes I alone—spent with Phil near the weir were some of the most deeply serene periods we spent on the Island. (This was due to Phil and his connection with the weir, but it may also have been the place, as I remember a long peaceful spring morning which we spent with Harold Turner there, the three of us lying on the grass at the head of the harbor.) I'm sure there are long periods of backbreaking work, but the pace of Phil's tending of the weir is nothing like the pace he keeps up when lobstering. It's evening work, after supper, a time of day which seems suited to going out in the skiff and seeing what is coming in from the great sea outside.

On the other hand, it isn't the time of day but the weir itself which seems to have a settling effect on Phil. I remember stopping by it with him one morning when he had just started out hauling lobster traps. He pulled up to the side of the pound to check something, and we paused and leaned over to watch the school of herring inside swim by in a mass, like people going down into the subway. Afterward, we sat for a while on the afterdeck, the boat lying gently by itself alongside the twine wall of the pound, and he told me about the school of little pilot whales he'd seen one day just a little out from the weir. He remembered that they were squeaking—"a whole lot of little fellers, looked like they was babies"—and he recognized them as what his father had called pothead whales because of the shape of their heads, and he looked them up and, sure enough, they were pilot whales. There was a moment of savoring the memory, and then we pushed off into the frantic pace of lobstering.

I think Phil is a very religious man—not so much because he is a vestryman of the church (although this is not a contradiction of the quality either) but because he has a deep belief in the natural order of things and in the rhythms of nature and is constantly amazed at his fellow creatures in whatever size or shape they come. Looking at a sea cucumber which had come up in a trap: "Now isn't that some strange! You wouldn't think a thing like that would be good for anything, would you? But I bet it is, if we only knew what." I remember one beautiful spring evening when Julie and he and I leaned against his truck in which he'd come down to check the weir, and he told us about a bird which had followed him all that day when he was out hauling, thought it was going to come right on board, wished I'd been there to photograph it. Later we looked it up, and Phil agreed that it was a shearwater.

Every once in a while there is a major scientific discovery which, instead of closing the gap between what we have known about something and what we think there is to know about it, expands our awareness of the outer limits of that subject. We discover that the more we know the more we are aware of what is unknown. That the mysteries of nature are infinite is a good working premise for scientists, photographers and the keepers of weirs, and Phil is constantly reaffirming this premise. "We thought the clams were all dug up [ten years ago], but the clams came back [as they have on the Island in the past couple of years]—something happened; we don't know what it is, but something happened." Out of deep experience Phil has come to the conservationist conclusion that when man tries to exploit nature like as not he messes things up—a conclusion which is not generally shared by his fellow fishermen, who are just beginning to question the belief that absolutely anything they can do to increase their share of the catch is worth the environmental damage. He believes that we don't understand nature, and that things are being used up. I agree with him, but *I* know about the arrogance of man in the face of nature mainly through a kind of political consciousness, whereas I think *he* knows it by waiting patiently by the weir for his share of the natural mysteries.

There is a short spring, starting about late May...

Flowering shad

Spruce buds

Violet among the rocks

Young skunk cabbage

Shad tree

... and then about ten weeks of summer

A gull watches from the top of the cliffs of the nesting island.

Blueberries
Wild rose

Black algae, barnacles and rockweed, situated in zones on the vertical
face of a rock according to the amount of time each can remain out of water.

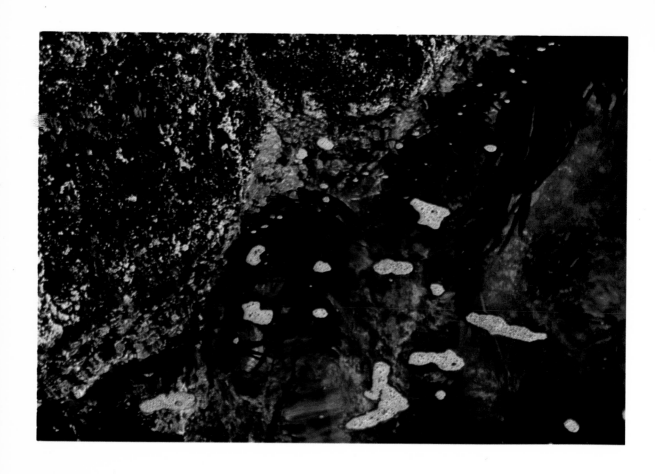

Detail of a tide pool

Periwinkles

Horse mussel

8

SUMMER

To many people, up until a few years ago, the name of the Island was synony-
mous with the name of the traditional summer colony (which I will continue
to refer to as the Point). The Point's beginnings were in the late 1870s, and its
founder was Ernest Bowditch, a young landscape artist from Boston of distinguished but not terribly wealthy family. In his old age (about 1916) he dic-
tated an account of his first visit, which says a great deal about the relationship
of the Point to the Island:

> Either in 1878 or '79 I went to Bar Harbor . . . [which was just starting its
> existence as an elegant summer place].
> Returning by the boat . . . I noticed to the southward the outline of a somewhat
> larger island standing up out of the sea, which was bolder and appeared more
> interesting than any of the others, with even the name of which I was unfamiliar.
> In answer to my question, "How do you get there?" the pilot said, "Don't
> know, but suppose you get off at [the Main] and charter a small boat."
> "Is there a hotel there?"
> "Don't know; don't know much about it, but kind of think if more people knew
> of it there might be fewer people go to Bar Harbor."
> This sounded interesting, and it being Friday afternoon only, I stepped off
> the steamer . . . and feeling like a combination of Christopher Columbus and
> Robinson Crusoe, chartered a small boat to go the remaining distance of six miles
> through the network of islands. . . .
> When somewhat more than one-half of the distance had been passed, the skipper

139

of the small boat . . . began a conversation, which was like this:

"Where was you goin'?"

"Going to the hotel."

"Ain't no hotel."

"Then take me to the village."

"Ain't no village."

"Where would you go if you were going to the town?"

"Shouldn't go."

"If you had to go where would you put up?"

"Well, if I *had* to go I s'pose I should get put up to Capt'n William Turner's—him as keeps the store."

"That is where I will go then."

"Can't get down to the store now 'cause it's low water, but I'll land you over to the old wharf [at the Point], and you can walk across the fields in a few minutes."

Accordingly I was landed near where the [Point] wharf is now built, and after a few minutes' cross-country walking—during which time I wet both feet—I reached the "store," which consisted of a corner of the old lobster factory that had been partitioned off with matched boards; and here I found sitting around a stove three or four old fishermen, who looked up at me as if I was some new and interesting marine animal. I inquired which of the number might be Captain William, at which one of them spoke up, asking what I wanted.

I asked whether he could keep me over Sunday, which he answered so abruptly in the negative that my vanity was hurt. Being at a loss what to do or say under these conditions, which had not occurred to me as possible, probably I hesitated and he added, "Say! what's your name?"

"Bowditch," I replied.

"That's a funny name; be you any relation to the fellow who wrote the *Navigator?*"

Then it occurred to me possibly to gamble on the family name, and I said further—"He was my grandfather."

"Your grandfather? You go right over there (pointing to a house) and tell the old woman you have come to make a visit."

Acting on this I presented myself at the old Squire Turner house, and announced to Mrs. William Turner that I had come to pass Sunday. This was not only my introduction to [the Island] but to a friendly intercourse that has continued for more than thirty years. Even today, no one on the island can be persuaded that I did not come as part and parcel of some deep laid plan that has not yet materialized —the idea of a chance visit being in their judgment very remote and improbable.

Mr. Bowditch's account goes on to ascribe his first cool reception by Captain Turner to the islanders' memory of Colonel Montgomery, the entrepreneur

whom I have mentioned in the first chapter as having built a dance pavilion
and cheated them out of land and lodging. After spending two days on the
Island, and having arrived at the usual appreciation of it, he returned to Boston,
and over the next year interested a group of his bachelor friends in forming
a syndicate to buy land there for their summer enjoyment. In the account he
states that his total capital at that time amounted to thirty-five hundred dollars,
which seems to indicate that the group was a lot less well off than the tycoons
who were settling their heavy selves into other areas of the Maine coast; on the
other hand, land was cheap, and before long they had increased the original
purchase of two or three hundred acres tenfold. They built a house for themselves on the foundations of Colonel Montgomery's old dance pavilion and
formed a club, whose rules excluded women, children and dogs. The rules were
quickly amended when the first of the bachelors got married, and the pace of
expansion picked up.

The account continues:

. . . Then a permanent wharf was needed, and that was built; then a laundry,
water works; a steamboat line subsidized, a new post office established in the Club
House itself and the road building started on the island. Until then there had been
nothing but trails.

The Club House proved insufficient in size, and it was suggested that the Directors
of the Company should each build a cottage and that the Club House be retained
for the entertainment of our guests. In a measure this was done, and today there is
the Club House, with dining-room and kitchen, of sufficient size to accommodate
sixty guests; eight cottages, besides servants' quarters, laundry, freight house,
ice houses, waiting room, wharf, steamer, numerous gas boats, row and sail boats,
sixteen miles of driving road, two daily mails per day, a livery stable, Memorial
Town Hall and Public Library, a new school house; and the Club House during the
season maintains a fisherman, resident physician, a milk farm and kitchen garden.
The arrivals at the Club are about three hundred each year.

He doesn't mention that most of the above facilities were connected by an
internal telephone system. It was quite a setup, and it is a measure of the grandeur of those times that this was modest compared to Northeast Harbor and
Bar Harbor, on Mount Desert.

The eight "cottages" were built by Clarence Turner, typically of shingle
which turned a rich gray in one year of weathering; boardwalks were built
connecting them with each other and the clubhouse for the preservation of long
skirts from the ravages of the huckleberry bushes. There is a smell which goes

142 with houses of this style and material—a special kind of pleasant mustiness— which only comes out in the summer, as I found out when I went into one of them in the middle of winter and returned in August. The Point then was bare of trees, as was a great deal of the Island, and the complex of massive structures must have looked ridiculously gargantuan only half a mile away from the settlement of frame buildings which made up the town. In the last twenty years trees have grown up, which are cut in such a way as to screen the Point buildings discreetly from the sight of vessels entering the Thoroughfare while allowing a view from the porches over the heads of these vessels to the beautiful distant reaches of the bay—like a one-way mirror.

The relationship between the Point and the Island remained as complicated as it had started. The islanders were not about to be overwhelmed by servants' quarters, steamers, laundries, liveries, town halls, public libraries, resident fish- ermen, milk farms and kitchen gardens. They had no complaints about the addition to the prosperity of the Island which the provision of such services meant, but they didn't take to the role of servitude, and I get the impression that this was fine with the Point people, who, after all, had settled here away from the centers of Maine summer society on purpose. They were there on the Island because it was a different environment from the one in which they lived during the winter even though they had provided themselves with one or two winter conveniences.

There was an economic-cultural gap between them and the islanders, but the separation of classes was more directly expressed then, and perhaps this made possible a comfortable interchange in which each group was able to maintain its own separateness comfortably and therein to find the common ground be- tween them. It also remained very clear to everybody just who had been on the Island first. The scraps of evidence of the winter-summer relationship which have come to me give an unclear picture. Mineola Rich worked as the managing housekeeper for the Point in the summer and, after her husband died, spent some winters in Boston working for her summer employers. Being a house- keeper in those days of closer attention to form and manner required the learn- ing and acceptance of elaborate ceremonies which might easily seem foolish to someone brought up on a Maine island. I understand that there was a certain amount of struggle between her and one of her employers on the question of the absolute necessity of daily changing the bedsheets so that the bottom and top sheets not only replaced each other but were reversed and turned so that the northeast corner became the southwest corner, and so on. It would have been

a lot harder for a Maine woman to accept such downright foolishness from an
employer than it would have been for, let us say, an Irish girl who had been
raised to accept the idiosyncrasies of the gentry, like the young Boston Irish girls
imported to wait on table at the clubhouse.

Professor William Turner's education at MIT was paid for by a loan made
after Ernest Bowditch had seen him take a watch apart and put it together
again; the loan was repaid. Helen Barter remembers that in the twenties Mrs.
Bowditch held a ball once a year to which the islanders came, and that everyone
wore long dresses. On the other hand, Maurice remembers that once, when he
and three others were drilling a hole into a rock—a process which involved one
man holding a diamond-faced bit and gradually turning it while it was driven
in by the successive sledgehammer blows of the others—Mrs. Bowditch went
by in her carriage, and he almost got clobbered as he turned to raise his hat.
Patronage, the role of the gentry—and yet, for example, I have the impression
that the Point people and the islanders were either on a mutual first-name basis
or else they addressed each other formally by their last names. One of Ernest
Bowditch's sons, William Bowditch, remembers, in a set of reminiscences I
found in the library, that Charles Turner, Harold's father, "literally showed me
everything I ever knew about boats" and that they sailed to Labrador together.
I'd guess that one paid the other but that, otherwise, it was a relationship of
friends and that the two men were held together by one wanting to learn what
the other one knew more than they were kept apart by one being richer and/or
formally better educated than the other.

I have a slightly clearer picture of life at the Point during the late thirties
and early forties because some of those who were then growing up there are
around now. The wives and children of the approximately eight families who
were members came for the months of July and August, and most of the fathers
came for two weeks, usually in August, and for occasional long weekends. For
about half of each day the kids were in the care of a tutor, who would be a
college boy hired specially to take care of them, teach them sailing, take them
on hikes and the like—a kind of small day camp—and, according to one partici-
pant, they all had a great time. On rainy, foggy days they played "murder" in
the old houses, which were admirably suited to this.

Luncheon and dinner were served in the main clubhouse by waitresses from
Smith College in yellow uniforms; this hiring practice continued into the fifties
and, remembering them, a faraway look comes into the eyes of certain of the
Island men who were young then; I imagine the college student tutors also re-

member the summers with pleasure—not to mention the Smith girls themselves. According to one source, you could dress informally at lunch, but not very. On Sunday evenings there was hymn singing in the clubhouse ("Oh hear us when we cry to Thee/For those in peril on the sea").

Katherine Butler and Rita Parker, two doctors who have been summer residents on the Island since 1931, have shared a few selected memories of those times with me. They ate at the clubhouse before their house on Birch Point (the northeast tip of the Island, about a mile from the Point) was built, and they remember fondly a Miss Fowler and a Miss Fry, who were great friends and came to the Point every summer together but were never heard to address each other as anything but Miss Fowler and Miss Fry. (I remembered that at about that time my sister was going to the girls' boarding school of which Miss Fowler had been the headmistress and the students' parting song of praise was fresh in her repertoire; all I can remember of it is the phrase ". . . to you, Miss Fowler, dear.") The doctors remember that Miss Fowler and Miss Fry would sit quietly at supper at their table in the dining room, each facing west for the sunset like a couple of elegant gulls on a bluff; they also remember the two ladies riding past Birch Point on their weekly circuit of the Island, seated formally in the back of Bill Robinson's cleaned-up lobster boat.

I'd guess that the doctors' social credentials were all right, but in the thirties the Point was still a pretty rarefied place. Out for a walk one day shortly after they moved to the Island, they met two ladies and continued in their company; after a moment one of the ladies peeked out from beneath one of those nice big floppy summer hats they wore then and asked Dr. Butler where she came from. "New York," replied Dr. Butler, to which Dr. Parker quickly added: "But she was born in Boston." Silence—and then: "And where are *you* from, Dr. Parker?" to which the reply: "New York." Longer silence and then, with a sigh of brave resignation: "I suppose one *can* live in New York." This sounds out of the funny papers, but I remember from my own childhood in Northeast Harbor, also on the Maine coast, that Main Line Philadelphians could fulfill even broader caricatures. We New Yorkers, on the other hand, were totally cosmopolitan.

The time to call was about 10 A.M. Ladies wearing white cotton gloves and three-quarter-length white coats would arrive and, if they found no one in, would leave calling cards. Finding such cards on their doorstep one day shortly after they moved into their house on Birch Point, the doctors quickly printed their names in ink on a few hastily cut rectangles of cardboard and made the rounds of the Point cottages to return the calls—only to find that everyone was out on a community picnic to which they hadn't been invited. By the late thirties the doctors were accepted despite their exotic winter address, and on their part, they had dug through the layer of manner to find really good friends. There were elegant tea parties on Birch Point which were timed to end before the arrival of the fast young crowd for cocktails; sometimes the first party would merge into the second.

All that time, during the thirties and early forties, there were other summer visitors who, by choice or social differences or a combination of both, had very little to do with the Point. Even in 1916 or thereabouts, according to the Ernest Bowditch account, there were "in the town six other summer cottages, and two —and sometimes four—of the townspeople take summer boarders." During one other of their early summers on the Island the doctors ate at the Turner boardinghouse in town with a small number of other summer people who had houses but chose to eat most of their meals out—including Justice (later Chief Justice) Harlan Stone. They particularly remember one evening meal when a guest of theirs went on at length about how much she loved clams and how many she could eat at one sitting, until the Justice was moved to remark that "it reminded him of the story about the woman who ate so many clams that her bosom rose and fell with the tide." A slight strained silence fell after the story, there at the Turner boardinghouse table, but it would have been totally inappropriate at the Point, which the Justice well knew. I have heard that he was one of those who, even then, came to the Island largely for a change in environment rather than to continue the regular environment of his winter life in a different physical setting. He obviously enjoyed the change in identification also. There is a story that he met the mailboat one day dressed in his usual manner, gave some people a lift to the Point and was told that the bags could go right upstairs, thank you; he took the bags upstairs.

If the Point had rigid standards of behavior, they were not terribly different from the standards of behavior of the year-round islanders. Most significantly, the Point was managed by people who ranked ostentation high in the list of sins and orderliness of manner and financial dealings high in the list of virtues. This may not seem to be reconcilable with the list of amenities which Mr. Bowditch lists earlier, but the Point was really primitive compared to the monuments to expansive capitalism elsewhere on the New England coast. Most of all, there was a determined Bostonian quietness which served to keep even the great shingled cottages from dominating the community in which they sat.

Mrs. Ernest Bowditch refused to allow the cruise of the Boston Yacht Club to return to the Point after there had been too much drinking one year in the twenties. In this she may have been strait-laced, but there was a lot more connection between the average fisherman and her at the moment of rectitude than there would have been between the fisherman and the drunken aristocrat whom she ejected—or even between herself and the drunken aristocrat (who might have come from right down the street at home).

Nothing is more anachronistic to the Maine coast than yacht clubs and the organized activities which accompany them; for example, there may have been a fishing community at Northeast Harbor or Bar Harbor before the mid-nineteenth century, but the remains are certainly not evident now, and that is the work of other characters than the late George Apley. As Mrs. Bowditch and, after her, her daughter persisted in the prohibition of a bar (and all which that implied then), the Point was kept from moving away from the Island community around it. Furthermore, there seems to have been a resistance among the Point people to social cohesiveness and, therefore, social exclusivity. The place was run more as a convenience than as a club; for example, the people in the cottages weren't particularly required by rule or custom to eat meals at the clubhouse, and many didn't; there was, as I've said, no bar and the only thing to do at the clubhouse on other than hymn-singing nights was to play billiards and talk.

What is really strange is that among people who sailed a great deal, there was no organized sailing regatta. They are a hard temptation to resist, as I found out when I lived in one section of Mount Desert which was filled with refugees from the social pressure of Northeast Harbor. It turned out that they were unable to go more than a few years without starting a regatta of their own, although they were aware that it was the first step to destruction and have tried to stay clean in their happy chaos by making light of the race. The Point held one sailing regatta during my first summer, but there was such a complete mixture of types of boats as to make handicapping, and therefore serious competition, impossible. We would have come in fifth and beaten a rather heavy old two-masted schooner if I hadn't fouled one of Jack MacDonald's lobster traps on the downwind leg.

During the war the Point was deserted, and by the end of the war the people who had dominated its life during the thirties were no longer around. There had always been a resident doctor each summer, as many of the members were too old to like having the nearest medical attention on the mainland if they could afford otherwise; and these few doctors from the old days, who had come to know the place, formed the nucleus of a new group. The doctors were used to less luxury, and the style of living changed. The laundry was converted into a residence, and only a few families brought their own servants, although the happy tradition of college-girl waitresses persisted. Wives and children tended to stay with their husbands at home for more of the summer, the cottages were empty for weeks at a time, and the shorter visits of the member families could not justify the cost of continuing even those services which remained.

Therefore, in the mid-fifties the Point advertised for paying guests to keep the clubhouse rooms and the cottages filled. I guess it was the most discreet whisper in the history of advertising. A brochure was printed, with phrases like ". . . is a club in that it reserves the right not to take all comers"; the houses were admitted to be self-sufficient but "in most cases it is found pleasant to plan to have a majority of meals at the club. For those who wish to be completely independent the club provides a commissary at which vegetables, fruit, milk, meats and fish may be obtained." The operation was so aristocratically conscionable that it couldn't even operate the typical company store of resorts in the usual monopolistic fashion and went on to admit that "purchases are possible at two small stores in the village." This hard-hitting piece of literature was mailed to the clients of an inn on the mainland which was so exclusive as to be almost underground, and an equally socko ad was placed in the pages of the *Junior League Magazine.* Later the management, squaring its shoulders in the interests of solvency, placed an ad in *Vogue,* but that was the most vulgar the whole exercise got.

In 1957 the club became an association whose function is to provide service for the original eight cottages and seventeen other summer houses: garbage pickup (James Myers, a college-student summer resident, had been sanitary engineer for a couple of years and by the time I came along had devised an eloquently expressed but tough set of rules for the proper packaging of garbage), the post office (Helen Barter), a wharf and set of sailboat moorings, generation of electric power (the Point has decided to hook up with the power company after its present generator wears out) and general maintenance (a full-time and busy three-month job for Bob Turner and a crew consisting of Harold van Doren and two men from the Main). The special boat which was run from the Point wharf to the Main has been replaced by a stop on the regular mailboat run during July and August—with a stern admonition from the summer mailboat captain to the day trippers that the wharf is private and that they are on no account to get off.

Some of the old traditions remain—the only truly Kiplingesque one being the firing of a sunset gun by one of the householders—but the Point has really ceased to exist as an institution and is now a physical collection of summer houses, most of them occupied by their owners for only a couple of weeks during the summer. It has been decades since it was the basis of the summer population in the sense of prestige or numbers, and the first summer I was on, it seemed like a tiny, tucked-away enclave in one corner of a lively, fairly complex summer social environment. The degree to which some of the Point people were isolated seemed to be borne out by the fact that Pat Tully found a check from one of them in payment of a gasoline bill, which had been slipped through the slot of the old store, as it should have been, but made out to Harold Turner, who hadn't run the gasoline concession for two summers.

I wandered around the Point a few times during the winter as well as the summer, and yet I would still get confused at boardwalk intersections on my way to visit people there at the end of August. Harold van Doren admitted to getting lost after he'd been working there every day for an entire month.

Things were starting to change dramatically that summer. Julie met a son of one of the Point families at the community painting of the schoolhouse and asked him how long he'd been coming "here," meaning the Island. He replied that he'd been here for only a couple of weeks, but that he'd been coming *there,* indicating the nearby Point complex with his paintbrush, for twenty-six years. There were a couple of parties at the Point easily and unself-consciously attended by all groups, more groceries were bought at the store by Point people who had previously done most of their shopping on the Main, and in general the Point householders were more visible outside the maze of boardwalks.

For me this new sense of unity reached a moving climax at the meeting between the Island and representatives of the park, which published a master plan threatening to transform the park from a relatively benevolent landlord of two-thirds of the island into a slumlord of an even larger acreage acquired by condemnation. The extent to which the drafters of the plan were familiar with local matters was demonstrated by a map which showed the route of a projected sightseeing boat trip around the Island as going outside of York Island through what is known as the Turnip Yard, possibly the foulest water in the whole bay. The other moves which were threatened didn't promise such easy disposition, and we were alarmed and angry. The important thing was that the two most eloquent speeches were made by a fisherman and by a direct descendant of the Bowditch who had given the park the land in the first place, and that the two speeches were from exactly the same point of view: that the future of the Island had to be determined by the people who lived there most of the time. The issues and interests were such that anywhere else I can think of there would have been some sort of broad group division between the summer and the year-round people, but here there was basically none. There seemed to be a direct line from that moment to Ernest Bowditch's meeting with Captain Turner ninety-four years previously.

By now the summer population (it could hardly be called a colony) is totally heterogeneous—a number of individual families held in a loose federation by virtue of the fact that they all come to the Island. Their winter occupations are absorbed into their identities as part of the whole community, and to me they are more summer islanders than anything else, but it may be useful to categorize them into universally recognizable groups. Making a rough estimate— and I mean rough, as I only knew them for a short time compared to the amount of time I knew the year-round people—I would guess that, out of the approximately fifty households which were on the Island for more than a week that summer, there were twelve doctors, ten academicians, nine executives and eight single women involved in various activities; there were four retired couples, three families from the Main (for example, the Cousinses), three clergymen, a couple of journalists, a U.S. senator and an architect. Since all of these avoid organized activity, as *summer people,* it is hard for me to see them as a group and therefore capable of subdivision, so there may be wild errors in the above. The high proportion of academicians—not to mention doctors— would indicate that it isn't a very wealthy group, although I would guess that there are a few who have a great deal of money, but you can't tell this by the fact that they live on the Island—you'd have to track down their winter lives to know. It's a mixed lot. I think there's a Nobel Prize winner who was on or maybe still is, but I don't know which one he is, or was. It isn't modesty, it's preoccupation. I guess I was the only one whose occupation was evident, by virtue of equipment and general nosiness and bustle.

Most of the summer people get absorbed into specific locales—town, the Point, Moore's Harbor, Head Harbor—and there are no places which are really acknowledged as centers. There is such a subconscious resistance to organization that if anyone ever acknowledged that the gang hung out in a certain place I'd expect that the gang would disintegrate. You could meet

150   people at the store (which in the winter is a meeting place by virtue of its being open for only an hour each day) and maybe at the dock at mailboat time, but you couldn't count on it. The pond, running down the east side for a mile and a half, was about as close to a gathering place as you'd find, and on sunny warm days there would likely be the Island version of the typical summer gathering of mothers and kids on the tiny beach at the southern end made several years ago from a truckload of sand.

The confusion of social types is staggering. The August 6 entry in my diary is indicative of this mix. It was a Sunday and after church there was a birthday party for and presentation of a silver platter to Miss Lizzie. (We had all sung a chorus of "Happy Birthday" at the end of the service, the church being Congregational and Miss Lizzie being special.) All of the churchgoers were at the party, both year-round and summer of course, and I guess the congregation was slightly larger that Sunday because we all knew about the celebration. Immediately afterward, there was a housewarming party for a summer house which had just been built by a couple who are related to a family so wealthy that its name is a synonym for wealth; I'd say that over half the people who were at the party when I was there were year-round islanders. There was no special consciousness of this intermingling. From the housewarming we went for a while to the community paint-in at the school, which was attended by a group consisting largely of young summer people, although there were a few year-rounders. We stayed there just long enough to get a little paint on our clothes as proof of virtue and then went off to a clambake at Moore's Harbor given by the summer residents there, which, thinking back, was about sixty percent year-rounder. Again, I emphasize that, although I'm doing a group breakdown, nobody, including me at the time, was particularly conscious of any special mingling of diverse types. This isn't sociological naïveté or utopia or anything like that; it's just that by now the lines between summer and winter islanders are quite blurred by crossover and, more than that, by the strength of the place itself.

Jim Kennedy, who was the first summer person—as a matter of fact, the first person of any kind—I met on the Island, told me that people asked him what he did all summer without the usual aids to enjoyment available in most resorts; he thought about it and realized that he couldn't come up with any clear answer. The fact is that what Jim and everyone else does is just live on the Island. The performance of daily necessities like going to the store or post office or hunting up someone to do something or answer a question fills a day the way standing under a maple tree in fall fills you with light. There are projects, but the projects are mainly excuses to be on the Island. The Island is physically beautiful, to say the least, but it is really the winter community which forms the basis of the lives of the summer people—the winter community felt as a presence if not known well individually, although most people on the Island do know each other well.

I even felt this in the most formal occasion of the summer. Invited to cocktails once in an easily elegant house (not on the Point) and meeting an elderly lady of aristocratic background, I felt very different than I would have felt in the same situation elsewhere. Our host and hostess and the lady were friendly and interesting, but I felt a formality which was unexpected and yet very pleasant. Despite whatever similarities in background there were between us, similarities which would normally have been used to find a common ground, there was little of that slurring of real meaning which is often the result of finding out that someone you've just met knows the code set of passwords to the club you belong to (political club, class or regional club, professional club, etc.). I felt we were all paying particularly close attention to each other and were not assuming that we knew each other's attitudes and therefore generalizing the relationship. Thinking about this afterward, I realized that we had met on ground which—even at a *cocktail party* if you can believe it—was so uncommon to our winter lives and yet so important to all of us that it, the Island, became the essential common denominator. We were each asking, "How did *you* get here?" as we would have asked each other if we had met in, say, Paradise. Another thing I noticed was that the formality—which is to say, the consciousness that the party was an *occasion*—reminded me of Island parties in the winter.

It became evident to me that the Island was probably the center of the lives of many of the summer people, including many people who, in the winter, led active lives and held positions of high responsibility. This was particularly, but not exclusively, true of the non-Point people. There was the natural pride in number of summers on the Island but also, sneaking in, the pride of being on close terms with the year-round residents. Certainly, as the place started to fill up in June, and as I told people who had been coming for many summers about life in the winter, I was aware of a certain loftiness in myself. There was no doubt in my mind, and perhaps very little in theirs, that I was nobler as well as enviable because of my winter visits; certainly I was temporarily one up.

But it is not just the perverse pride of being familiar with an exotic place and its customs which puts a premium on connection with the year-round community; much more, it's the sense that the islanders are special people whom it's an honor to know, and a sense among many of the summer residents that, when it comes right down to it, they themselves *are really* better for having spent summers here—both *because* they came and as a result of having come.

Bill Kirk, who lives in town, experienced enough sense of acceptance to last a man a lifetime when he returned to the Island after an absence of twenty-five years and was welcomed by Skeet MacDonald. He let the boat he was in lie off the town float a ways and asked Skeet, who was in a punt next to the float, if he could tie up. Although he recognized Skeet, Skeet didn't quite place him and, after saying that most everybody tied up there and it was fine by him, asked whom Bill was visiting. When Bill mentioned the name of his friends, Skeet recognized him and held out one hand in greeting while, with the other, he pushed off from the float, saying simply, "Welcome back." After a moment like that you tend to stick around a bit—as Bill and Mary have.

On a more serious level, Katherine Butler remembers that once, when J. K. Barter, who kept the store then, was filling the tank of her banana wagon, he happened to glance down and, removing the cigar from his mouth, remarked: "Them's a good pair of legs. You wouldn't think an old rooster like me would notice things like that, but I do." I'm sure she said something like "Why, Mr. Barter!" but she still remembers it as a real compliment as much as she remembers it as a story of a nice old eccentric.

In short, most of the summer people have varying degrees of intimacy with various year-round islanders, according to their various natures, but it is also true that the islanders represent the place and for this are honored by the summer people. Generally, I know this is true to my experience of the Island in memory, now that I am not even spending odd weeks during the winter on it and therefore, in a way, have returned to the condition of a summer visitor. The islanders have become more than a group of friends from whom I'm separated —they are a distant noble race. I realize that this may be the result of doing a book, but I wouldn't be surprised if this heightening of reality takes place among many of my summer neighbors.

It's easy for me to understand now why I was treated with a certain amount of restrained hostility when I started to make preliminary visits that August (apart from the real danger that my identification of the Island might serve as an advertisement for more visitors, which is the last thing the place needs). Because the summer people know that the admission policy is ultimately in the hands of the year-rounders, as is right and proper, there is a certain pride in belonging to the community, and certain warnings against trespass are displayed to the visitor: one lady who has been coming on practically every summer of her life advised me, quite appropriately, that one could spend an entire generation getting to know the Island, and when I answered in the vernacular: "You can say that again," she replied: "And I will!"

On their part, the year-round residents look on the individual summer visitors whom they like as real friends, with all the joys and complication which that implies, and think of them less as a group than even they themselves are thought of as a group by the summer people. Being oriented to summer visits to Maine, I expected that during the long winter evenings, there would be a certain amount of wistful recounting of the eccentricities of summer life. I don't remember hearing much, and I don't think that was because I was doing a book. Rather, fall, winter and spring is a period nine months long, and a lot can happen to cause the summer to recede. I can remember once that sometime in spring I made a comment to Maybel Chapin in the store about its soon being time for the annual migration, and she made it clear to me in pleasant but no uncertain terms that the Island likes its summer visitors and, for more than economic reasons, welcomes their return as individuals and does not think of them as an invading horde.

As the Island is two-thirds park, there is a crowd of visitors arriving almost daily during July and August. They divide up into day trippers, who come out on the morning mailboat and return on the afternoon trip, and campers. The campers are no particular problem to the community, as they have had to make reservations at the Duck Harbor campground, sometimes months in advance, and Bill Stevens meets them at the boat, checks them in and sets them on the four-mile hike down to Duck Harbor. The campground consists of four shelters (three walls and a roof) holding a total of sixteen campers, outdoor fireplaces and a couple of outhouses.

However, the day trippers *are* thought of as an invading horde, and conflicts do occur between them and the community. There are no public overnight accommodations except the campground, so they have about four hours on the Island, which is too short a visit to begin to walk to the pond or the trails down at the southern end and too long a visit to be filled by visiting the church and the store. The Island could make a little money off the day trippers—Lord knows there is not much to do, as you don't dare take an extensive walk for fear of missing the return boat—and a lot of people end up down at the wharf with time on their hands and could be sold a few native trinkets or something. Although there is sometimes talk about this, nothing has been done—I suspect because there is a feeling that this would imply an acceptance of tourism which would open up the floodgates completely.

After that first trip in the chartered boat long ago I next experienced the Island as a day tripper and, given the special knowledge that I was going out to a place which would be my primary concern for the next two years and very carefully suspending the disclosure of that special fact (suppressing the urge to step off the boat and announce my presence in a loud voice), I felt quite strange as Julie and I and a few other strangers sat properly among the summer island-ers who lounged about the mailboat with enviable familiarity—new boys among the upperclassmen. Debarking, I had to go to the bathroom and encountered the usual first problem of the Island visitor. There is a sign which indicates a public toilet down the road in the opposite direction from what is clearly the "center" of town, but this public outhouse is situated on the nearest piece of park land—a little island of property surrounding the ranger's trailer—which is a couple of hundred yards away, and after walking fifty yards and not finding it, I decided, like most other visitors, that I was the victim of a cruel hoax and didn't have to go to the bathroom much anyway. From time to time, others have a more urgent need and give in to an indiscretion which, along with littering, seemed to be a pervasive irritant the summer I was on.

We walked through town smiling effusively—the way I remember doing in small European villages which I wanted to photograph and so had walked into with studied casualness, having parked my car just outside so as to enter, as it were, unarmed (which, naturally, didn't fool anybody). Arriving at the store, we bought a sandwich from Jean Deveraux's father at the sandwich concession which he was operating that year out of a window opening onto the store porch. After lunch, we walked halfway up the mountain so that I could go to the bath-room without fouling our future nest. Everyone had been pleasant to us, but I was most aware of being closed off from this complex natural and social beauty by the fact that I wasn't sure how to begin experiencing the Island and, indeed, wasn't sure if I could begin at all in the interval before the last boat left. Ad-mitted that my visit was loaded with special conditions, but still I can imagine others feeling the same way. It's a nice place to live, but I wouldn't want to visit there.

It's only in the past few years that the casual visitors have become too much, and, of course, this is just the same thing that has been happening all along the

Maine coast. The old attitude is expressed in the language of a sign at the beginning of the road leading out to the Lighthouse, which is now privately owned:

This is private property—not government property. Enter if you wish. You are certainly welcome but please be considerate.

Do not smoke or light fires

Do not enter the buildings

Do not touch anything

Do not litter

Please stop out to the Farmhouse to say hello before going to the Lighthouse.

Thank you

As their numbers increased, the day trippers provided income and diversity. Noyes MacDonald drove them around the Island for hire for several summers, and after a while he found himself making up wild stories out of boredom with answering the same questions—like saying that the tiny dirt road to the Cliffs led to a car ferry to a nearby island. Harold van Doren tried it for part of a summer but felt foolish sitting on the front of the car saying, "Taxi, taxi," at each mailboat arrival and arguing about the price of the trip, and he gave it up.

There are indications that the middle of the winter might be the best time to visit the Island casually. A young college student came on in February a few years ago and spent a few days by himself down at the Duck Harbor campground, after which he showed up at the post office, and Miss Lizzie gave him a hot meal and a place to sleep inside; they still correspond. Bill and Mary Kirk, who are on the Island a lot in the winter, although they live in New York, met a young couple walking around one bleak December day and having asked them in for tea discovered that they had camped on one of the porches at the Point the previous night. It turned out he was a Ph.D. from Columbia and the London School of Economics and, after a pleasant conversation about academic matters, they left for their second night on the empty Point porch, having politely refused Bill and Mary's offer of a bed. The Kirks became absorbed in something or other and didn't notice that the first blizzard of the year had started outside, until there was a knock on the door, which Bill opened to discover two white-encased figures in a white-encased world. Perhaps they could have stuck it out if they hadn't been reminded by the warm tea and conversation that they weren't really in the middle of the wilderness and that there were alternatives to their porch.

The summer I was on there was the incident of the attempted robbery of the store which I've mentioned, and the summer before, the Cousines' camp had been broken into and lived in for five days in such a manner that it took about a month of weekends to get the place cleaned up. The Island is big enough so that once someone has come on in the mailboat, he can just disappear accidentally or on purpose, living off his own supplies or, in this case, an empty house. The break-in hadn't been noticed because the men had kept up the tent which they had pitched across the road at Boom Beach and had stayed in until the Cousinses left. Anywhere else—even on the Main—it would not have been a particularly unusual event, but here it meant that this aspect of the outside world had caught up with the Island. Perhaps too readily, people began to lock their doors when they went off for a few days, and whereas before there had been a sort of informal system of checking whether the same number of people as came on the morning mailboat left on the afternoon trip (or else were accounted for as somebody's guests or official campers) for their own protection against being in trouble in the woods, now this same informal daily check tended to be made for the protection of the Island. If you think about it, it makes a big difference in a small place. In the same way, the one incident of aggressive nude bathing that same summer by a number of visitors at the "beach" at the end of the pond where everybody goes seems like a ridiculously innocent affront to local mores—again until it's realized that the Island is, by its nature, small and contained and so has more of a right to have its singularities respected than would a mainland place. The islanders have chosen to be off by themselves, have assumed the responsibilities of a host, and therefore ought to be treated with equivalent respect.

By now the Island's welcome of the casual visitor is hesitant. I discovered this when I took Julie to the Main in our own boat once in early summer for a special trip to New York and was about to return to the Island when a couple of young men who had arrived at the wharf on their bikes, soaked by the rain which had been falling all afternoon, asked me about the mailboat. There was a bit of maneuvering after I told them that the boat runs were through for the day and they asked me if I was going back over in my own boat and could take them. I obviously could, but they hadn't even heard of the campground much less made a reservation and, as a matter of fact, had intended to ask permission to camp out on someone's property. This was such a reasonable intent that I felt bad about hesitating and didn't know how to explain in under fifteen minutes, standing on the wharf in the rain, the entire history of the Island's mild ethnocentricity without having it sound like an excuse for meanness.

The upshot was that I took them over and they spent the night with me (as

I'd had an idea they would end up doing). I'd gone to find Bill Stevens, the ranger, to book them into the campground if there was any room, only to remember as I got to his trailer that he'd left that day for cop school (riot-control training for rangers). I had then located Pat Tully, his deputy, who signed them into the campground, only to come to the conclusion, as the downpour continued, that it was a lot simpler to put them up myself than drive them to Duck Harbor for half an hour over the dirt road on a rainy night and then drive back. Pat's disapproval of my bringing on unregistered campers was evident, even though they were only planning to spend the night and there was room at the campground. I came to the conclusion that, if I was going to be so damn hospitable again as to give people rides over, I'd have to go the whole course, rather than turn them over to the public responsibility. It was a further—and complicated—lesson in community living.

9

SUMMER INSTITUTIONS
AND EVENTS

CHURCH

Summer brings a whole set of special events to the Island, and even some
special summer institutions—like church.

According to one account, religious services were first held on the Island when
the mainland Baptists united with the islanders to support a ministry in the
early part of the century. By mid-century it had been decided to build a church:

At the earnest solicitation of the Ladies Sewing Circle . . . Rev. Joshua
Eaton, missionary here, set out on a soliciting agency to collect funds for building
a meeting house for the worship of God on [the Island], and taking passage
aboard the schooner ''Priscilla,'' Capt. Ezra Turner, March 27, 1855 bound for
Gloucester, Mass., meeting with head winds were 9 days on the passage.

The funds were collected, and the Union Congregational Church was dedicated
in 1857 on a May day which I like to think of as bright enough for the sun to
have struck brilliantly off the golden cod on its weathervane and calm enough
to have sent far and wide the sound of its bell, which had been salvaged from an
English bark wrecked a few years previous on a particularly blessed shore near
the Eastern Ear. In 1859 a pew assessment was voted as necessary "for extin-
guishing the debt and keeping the House in suitable repair and in necessary

condition for public worship—always excepting one fourth of the pews and seats in the body of the church to be free." Lest it be thought that the early congregation was a bunch of fuzzy-minded do-gooders, I would add that in 1887 it was voted that the sexton of the church be paid $1 a week, "if we cannot get him for 75¢."

Since then (with one remodeling in 1966 to repair the steeple, which, according to one person, was supported by termites holding hands) the church has stood resolutely as a landmark, visible for miles out to sea in some directions. It's unclear to me just how many of the late-nineteenth-century years it was functioning the year round, but it probably served as an ecumenical base for visiting clergymen in all seasons. A baptism by *total* immersion is recorded as having taken place on *December 26,* and I have seen photographs from sometime between 1885 and 1890 of Mrs. Alfarata Rich being baptized by the Baptist Elder Brewster in the waters of the Thoroughfare, which are not to be entered without a gasp even in the middle of the summer.

The fact that there was a summer ministry of divinity students in the early part of this century would seem to indicate that there was no winter minister at that time, as a minister who had suffered the winter would surely have taken the reward of the summer. I've quoted the entries of the diary of one of these young men, Willard Palmer, and another of the entries may give some idea of the difficulties of operating a seasonal ministry:

Wed., July 2 . . . At the close of the meeting we organized a young people's society with fourteen members. Most of them were girls from the Clubhouse [the Point] and will be of no permanent value of the society. My hope is to develop a society that will continue to hold meetings after the church services close, but there seems to be nobody here who can lead such a society, and I cannot expect to train up leaders in two months.

I don't know whether he ever complained out loud about this, but if he did I can almost hear an Island lady replying with something like: "Don't you worry none, Mr. Palmer, we'll be right here when you get back next summer." The Island absorbs everything, even evangelical fervor.

From 1913 to 1926 the Island enjoyed the luxury of a permanent minister and a permanent doctor in the person of one man, Frank Snell. Dr. Snell is mentioned as having even amputated the leg of a woman who wanted him to do the operation rather than go on the arduous trip to the mainland hospital.

The church is open now only in the summer, and in the last six years the minister has been Ted Hoskins, who succeeded his father in the job. His mother (our winter landlady) is organist. Ted grew up on the Island in the summer, he went stop seining for a while with Minot Connery, Gooden Grant and Charles Turner, Harold's oldest son, and I'd guess that he thinks of the Island now as his real home, even though his winter parish is elsewhere; as I've said, he stayed on during the winter of 1970–71 as schoolteacher. He's one of those clergymen who see themselves as social catalysts as well as spiritual comforters, who take seriously the deep moral crisis in this country and are not reluctant to push a bit. Early in the church season he gave a sermon on the value of excess, reminding the congregation that Jesus went beyond the laws of society; he was certainly aware, as I was just beginning to be, that abhorrence of excess is deep in the Maine ethic. The first formal suggestion of the power company had come from him one Sunday two years previously, he had pushed the idea of an Island planning committee more than anyone else, and he regularly held weekly discussion groups throughout the summer which really got issues of vital local concern talked about, despite the usual reticence at the outset of each one. A lot of the year-round and summer islanders met at these, and I have an idea that they may prove to have cut short the long road to the solution of problems which are now escalating too fast to be taken care of by the usual process of Island communication and politics. What was really impressive to me about Ted was that he was so perfectly attuned to the pace of the Island that he knew pretty much what action was possible in what length of time on any issue without running the danger of tearing the place apart.

Although you can't be too sure about these things (God, as Einstein said, is a Sly One), it was probably the church as an expression of the community, more than anything else, which brightened our Sundays. I've been a renegade from the Episcopal Church for a long time, and Julie was brought up a devout atheist, so any church service, and certainly the easy informality of the Congregational service (Ted in a suit, requests for specific hymns by the congregation during the service, announcements of community activities like dances, and so on) was new to us. After a childhood and adolescence of painful boredom in church, I was shocked to find myself looking forward to the Sunday service (although

I notice that I've been able to resist the temptation since I came back from the Island).

The sacramental highlights that summer consisted of six baptisms (with varying reactions from the babies to Ted's luxuriant beard), the confirmation of Ben MacDonald, who was going to high school off-island in the fall, and the formal joining of the church by Collie Heline, the wife of a fisherman. Especially, there was the marriage of Wendy Heline to Paul Sewall, a young fisherman from the Main. After the wedding there was a reception at the town hall. The guests left on the mailboat; the groom rowed out to his lobster boat and brought it in; and the bride, having changed into dungarees and taken off her shoes, climbed down the ladder into it, and the wedding party roared off, leaving the mother of the bride weeping among the propane tanks which are generally stacked along the wharf.

A few years back, there was what is known in the trade as a "walk-in wedding"—that is, one which takes place at the request of a couple of strangers who just arrive at the church wanting to be married. In this case, it was a couple of campers who had come onto the Island and had been so affected by the place and each other that they decided to get married. (I mean, when you find such a nice church to get married in, you might as well get married.) Ted scheduled the wedding for the next Sunday so that they could go back to the Main to get their license and spend the required period of residency before they returned to be married. He announced the wedding during the service, and the congregation, none of whom knew the camper couple, stayed for it. Someone went out and picked a bouquet of daisies for the bride; someone else went and got a cake; and a proper wedding was improvised, complete with loving guests. It would be a cruel irony if *that* marriage hadn't worked out.

The church fair and the church supper have traditionally been the main sources of church income—only slightly supplemented by the weekly collection. In 1896 the fair was held in the old lobster factory and grossed $86.50; our first year on the Island, it was held in the town hall (which hadn't been built in 1896) and grossed over a thousand dollars. The wares and activities were the same—for example, fir (balsam) pillows and cake-weight guessing. For weeks members of the congregation had been cutting the needles off fir branches, which they then stuffed into hand-embroidered pillow slips.

That summer the church supper took place separately; 225 people were fed (ham and baked beans, mostly), and the effort of feeding them was not to be believed. I went into the kitchen to photograph and knocked over and broke a bottle of syrup. Betty Barter turned to Julie and said: "Madam, would you please take your little boy out of here."

DANCES

The Island has always dearly loved a dance. Fifty years ago, word of the arrival of the fiddler would spread fast, and people would walk the three miles over the mountain from Head Harbor or row over from York Island or ride bicycles or drive teams of horses over the dirt tracks to converge on the old lobster factory, on the upper floor of which the dances were held. Maurice Barter can remember Freeman Hamilton (whom I earlier mentioned as having almost drowned with Gustus Rich) walking the three miles over two mountains from Duck Harbor and walking back, starting out from town about midnight.

Our first summer the dances were held in the town hall almost every Saturday night, and the dancers ranged in age from one-year-old Karen Wilson to ninety-six-year-old Gooden Grant. Gooden says he hasn't missed a dance in a long time, that he always pretty nearly managed to get over from Head Harbor by whatever means of transportation was being used at any particular point in the long span of his life, and he remembers running a boat between the Main and the Island to bring people over specially for the dances. He told me that he sometimes thinks he oughtn't to go to dances because he imagines that the young folks don't like to see him sitting there, meaning, I suppose, that a bent old man might seem out of place. I haven't taken a survey, but I can't imagine that he could be more wrong; to me he's an incentive to longevity, as I can think of few ways to be better entertained if I manage to get anywhere near his age than by sitting around at the Island dances. Occasionally he gets up and dances himself, and he's a mite bent over but you can tell he's danced some in his life.

Mostly the music is to work up a good sweat to—waltzes, interspersed with polkas, and occasionally just running around in vague time to the music by the younger kids. It was provided by a local pickup band consisting of Collie Heline, fisherman's wife, on guitar; Archie Hutchinson, fisherman, alternating with Bernadine Barter, fisherman's wife, on accordion; Bob DeWitt, Bishop of Pennsylvania, on sax; Noyes MacDonald, retired fisherman, on piano. By and large, I'd say they were the best dances I've ever been to. The high point of each one was the "Lady of the Lake," a square dance which I was unable to learn even after one month of not only practice at the dances but private coaching sessions with diagrams. When the conservation kids were on the Island clearing up the trails, they had a special practice session down at their camp on Eli's Creek before one dance; Ted Hoskins, who always called, was in good voice, and the "Lady of the Lake" was a joy to behold that night, as it was on another night when, for some reason, all but the experts dropped out and I had a chance to see at close hand the centrifugal force which is developed when one good Lady of the Laker meets another in a swing-your-partner. Miss Lizzie doesn't dance it any more, but several people have told me that she could generate enough power to send you into orbit if you didn't hang on.

BASEBALL

The Island baseball season opened the last Sunday in April. The field is right behind town.

During July and August, in good weather, there was likely to be some action around the field about six o'clock in the evening, although there was nothing organized. I didn't get there much, but Nancy Woolen, a summer resident who was there pretty regularly, told me that there was a wonderful chemistry which worked some evenings to create a baseball game or a soccer game suddenly out of a random group of kids and a few grownups hanging loosely about. Sometimes this chemistry failed to work, the adults drifted off, and the evening degenerated into an apple fight, but more often teams were chosen as if by magic out of what seemed to be quiet chaos, and a game got going.

YORK ISLAND—SHEEP

Except when the thickest fog hides it totally, York Island is a persistent part of the scenery of Rich's Cove. The mile-long island lies about a half mile off the shore of the Island and runs parallel to it. The northern half is wooded, and the southern half is rolling pasture with elegant clumps of tall spruce—the meadowland reminding people of western Ireland. What with one thing and another, I didn't get out to it until summer, which was frustrating because I kept hearing about its past. At one point the island was settled and photographs from the turn of the century show the harbor full of vessels. There was

Bob Turner on the mound, Gerri Turner at
second base, Maybel Chapin at shortstop

Harold Turner

Harold van Doren and Annie Haynes

Danny MacDonald

The author (sneaky photograph by Bill Barter)

Bob Turner, Jr.

York Island harbor, around 1910

a general store and what Phil called (easily—as an integral part of his vocabulary) a "fish stand," which he then had to describe to me as a structure used for salting away fish in vats. From about 1915 until recently the island was used almost entirely by off-island lobstermen for its good harbor, from which they could easily haul the traps which they set nearby in the summer and where they could hold lobsters in pounds until the market was right for selling. There are still two cabins on the island, which, for cabins on remote islands around here, are in excellent condition—meaning that the walls are more or less perpendicular, that there are a floor, glass in the windows, a roof and a stove which probably works. They're not used by lobstermen any more—with today's powerful motors it isn't necessary to camp near where you haul—but Julie and I found evidence of pretty recent occupation in the remains of contemporary groceries. In June the camps sat in their decrepitude in the lush meadows—disorder among the order.

York has been used for sheep grazing for as long back as sheep were raised on the Island, probably the early nineteenth century. Dennis Eaton kept about seventy there as late as the sixties and built the barn and the fencing which makes up the pen and the leads into it. Before that, Jim Connelly grazed about a hundred, and Harold Turner remembers helping to round them up for shearing and Connelly laughing like hell as two of his young helpers were dragged from one end of the island to the other by a ram they hadn't kept properly under control.

Connelly sold the island to a summer woman who, probably because York had the unique beauty of sheep pasturage, made a deal with Wayne Barter to continue the grazing—the deal being that she and Wayne would own the sheep jointly but that he would keep the proceeds from the wool and would do all the work. Wayne is in his late twenties, is the son of Irville and Dot Barter and Maurice's nephew. He lives on the Island, all except the three midwinter months, with his wife, Betty, who comes from Massachusetts, and their two little girls. Primarily he goes hauling with his brother, Bill. He and his family live in a new ranch house on the east side, which they built two years ago after Wayne got out of the army. For the last two years they've lived off-island in the winter months, because, what with the two little girls, one an infant, they didn't want to run the risk of being cut off from immediate medical attention. This winter Bill is going scalloping, and Wayne will go with him—which means one more precious couple with children for the life of the Island.

Wayne had helped his grandfather shear on Burnt Island; I imagine he saw it as something he knew, that was part of his past—and that he might as well continue, as he modestly put it, to give it a try. I bet that, if he wasn't an islander, he wouldn't have done it, no matter how much support was given by the owner of the pasturage; on the Main it would have seemed frivolous, not getting on with it. The complicated factors that impel Wayne and Betty to live on the Island despite the attendant difficulties of making a living are the same reasons that Wayne continues the sheep operation of his grandfather. Payson, his nephew (Bill and Bernadine Barter's son), is helping him, and Payson will be hard put to it in later years to avoid grazing and shearing sheep. No matter what happens to him, he's hooked; there will always be the memory of the joy of a skill just learned and the first feeling of adult function.

Forty years ago Phil Alley and his friends herded sheep on another island near where he grew up for two dollars a day of hard running. Nobody used sheepherding dogs then, and they don't now because they are too expensive to train for an occupation which is only supplementary; watching Payson tear over the tricky terrain of the York Island pastures, avoiding the rocks deep in the thick grass which were constantly threatening my aged ankles, I felt that he was as good as any border collie—which is saying a lot.

Actually some of the sheep had been sheared already that summer. The year before Wayne started grazing himself, the owner had given permission to a group with a name like Environment Action or something to camp on York and shear, and, being environmentally active and not in perfect communication with the owner, they had returned the next year to do what by then was Wayne's job. Wayne was obviously reluctant to speak about it, but I gathered that there was some kind of settlement.

I learned about the shearing when Wayne and Payson came down to Rich's Cove one foggy morning and rowed over to York to repair the fencing. The sheep stay on the island all winter, being hardy, and live primarily off rockweed, a diet which Wayne thinks is the reason they are completely free of worms. As sheep do, they travel together, but they're pretty wild, and we'd noticed on our previous trips to York that they tended to stay away from us—perhaps after their run-in with the amateur shepherds who had been there earlier. The general plan Wayne had for getting them into the pen by the old barn which Dennis Eaton had built was to drive them from the wooded northern half of the island to the bare southern half and then back into a ravine leading into the funnel of fencing which made up the mouth of the pen. The job of driving had been a lot simpler on Burnt Island when he was a boy, because that island has a narrow waist, and as the sheep tend toward its bare eastern end, they can be driven directly toward the funnel-like leads with no chance of their making end runs. On York it was like those vicious little games where you have to get a number of steel balls in a little plastic box around complicated barriers and into an enclosure within the box by rocking it this way and that. The sides of the ravine weren't so steep that a frightened sheep couldn't try to climb them and get hopelessly stuck, and the mouth of the ravine lay at almost right angles to the shore, so that if the sheep didn't turn as they were supposed to they would naturally go out onto the seaweed-covered intertidal rocks, where they could just stand and laugh at us in a frightened sort of way.

About six of us made the first attempted roundup, going over in my boat about six o'clock one morning. We split up, three of us to locate the sheep on the northern wooded end and drive them south, two of us hanging casually around the entrance of the ravine and one of us photographing. At the last moment they made an end run up the side of the ravine as they were about to enter the leads. We gave up, as it was a hot day, and Wayne was loath to drive them any more. It turns out that sheep can't be driven too hard or they will just drop dead. The one that got stuck in the rocks and was caught just lay there exhausted, as if resigned to some rule of the game which required her to give up and stay prisoner after she was tagged. It seemed a strange contrast to her considerable speed and hardiness.

Another—a lamb which dropped behind the escaping flock—was found to have no hind feet, a birth defect. I had the strange sensation of having the romantic generalization of lamb shattered by the hard specific of *this* lamb in *this* place, and I felt helpless. Avoiding the inevitable, Wayne put the lamb into the pen to be freed with the rest after the shearing. Later, after we got back, he reconsidered, and we saw him and Maurice set off to the island, Maurice carrying his rifle. Maurice said he pointed it at the lamb carefully so that he could turn away when he pulled the trigger.

I guess it was because this was his first drive on York Island, and he was willing to experiment, that Wayne, against his better judgment, agreed to the general plan of getting as many people as possible out there the next day so as to be able to line the ravine's sides and block the little passes up which the sheep could escape. Accordingly, about twenty men, women, children and infants—most of them summer residents—showed up at Rich's Cove at six o'clock the next morning to be taken across to the island in two shifts. The word had gotten around quickly, as it does, and even though I'd carefully told a couple of people to check with Wayne and they had, I regretted that I'd in-flicted a rabble on him. And a rabble we were when it came to driving, although all of us were willing and some of us were very pretty. Elthea Turner watched the operation through field glasses from her house across the York Island Passage, and she said it was as good as a movie—sheep in profile running across the top of a ridge, then a human figure, then more sheep.

The initial stage of the operation, getting them to the southern half of the island, was successful, and a sizable bunch was herded toward the ravine with all of us lining the walls like so many Apaches waiting in ambush. Just as the sheep were about to enter the fence leads into the pen and be trapped by the entire crowd roaring down behind them, the lead ram found the weak spot in the east defensive line and charged through to safety. The weak spot was

Sharon Wilson, who was carrying her year-old baby and was therefore handicapped. It is a measure of our intensity that Sharon felt guilty.

We retired for an hour to let the sheep and those who had been doing the running rest and lay around in the empty pen like a French Impressionist painting. After a while Wayne sheared the one sheep which someone had managed to tackle and hogtie, and most of us went and watched it lying calmly after the chase while the amazingly thick, lanolin-slippery blanket of wool was cut off. We manned the walls of the ravine again, and Mark Connors even moved an enormous cable spool which had washed up on the beach into a position inside the ravine where he could hide and cut off any divergence early on. After a time the main bunch came through our lines, heading south into the ravine as they should have, only to scatter onto the rocks in the low-tide area instead of turning back north into the leads.

In the end, five which hadn't been sheared earlier were caught and tied down. None had been penned and we dilettantes went back to the Island mainland. A couple of hours later I came back to get Wayne and his basic crew and about forty pounds of wool in a long burlap bag, which we threw aboard the boat. Wayne would take it to the mainland in a few days, where he expected to get eighty cents per pound for it, including the government subsidy paid both him and the sheepherding magnates of the West. I asked him if he was satisfied, and he paused, grinned and said he'd have to be, he guessed; I would have felt better about the operation if I hadn't thought of all that summer talent scattered about. I think this was on Wayne's mind too when he wondered out loud on the way back whether any of them had had a good time.

Next year he'll move the holding pen down into the ravine, extend one fence lead down to the water with a portable fence to take care of the low-tide zone and replace the rabble army with a few swift types like Payson. He also plans to sell most of the rams that are on York already (three out of the five sheared that day were males) and service the ewes with the Dorset ram he had in a pen near his house. In that way he can regulate the time of lambing so that the lambs will be born in clement weather in the woods. We found the skeletons of a couple of lambs that hadn't made it through the winter.

In the heat of the battle words like *fiasco* had occurred to me and I had images of Wayne as Napoleon at Waterloo. On reflection, however, it became clear that the peculiarities of the York Island terrain demanded that he try new techniques as well as study the literature and remember what he'd learned from his grandfather, and now, at least, the living-wall-of-summer-people technique could be discarded. It could only have happened within the easy pace of the Island.

10

FUTURE

Having spent most of my waking hours for the last year and a half in loving consideration of the Island—while actually there or back in New York—one would think that I would have some clear idea of its future, if not a downright prediction. However, all I have at hand is a sense of the most apparent problems which it faces and the strengths by which it will probably overcome these problems. I must admit to the romantic notion that the Island has an identity, apart from its people, animals, trees, rocks and waters; therefore, having arrived at this point in *its* time, and only at this point, I would feel arrogant making prophecies. If by magic I had known it seventy years ago at the height of its bustling prosperity, I would be depressed by what I know of it now. Now, it seems great, and I sometimes feel that I could wish for no more than the stabilization of its present condition, but there are grave problems which are getting worse. Maybe there were other, graver problems before this, about which we have no idea; I can imagine that, perhaps, the clams gave out one year during the time the Indians came every summer, which would have seemed pretty disastrous to them.

More than anywhere else, the seat of the Island's soul is its year-round community (in which I include those who go off for the three midwinter months) and the basic problem is the threat to its survival. This has been the basic problem for many years now as the population has diminished from its peak early in the century. By "community" I mean just that—a group of people 173 living most of the time on the Island and making their livings on it and from it or from its waters. I don't mean a retirement community, even if such a community could maintain itself without young people—which it couldn't. Nor do I mean a community or caretakers, waiting for the annual arrival of its summer-resident and day-tripper patrons (who, of course, would be different from the present summer residents, who come here because of the year-round community as much as anything else). Nor do I mean a bedroom community of people who work on the mainland and who might, with improved boat transportation, be able to commute daily. If the basic population degenerated into any of these states, there would be left only the physical Island, and, without a community with strong enough roots to protect it, that would probably go too after a while.

There is an enormous land boom on the Maine coast now. A retirement, summer or even a commuter population would resist the pressure of real-estate exploitation because they would tend toward natural conservation, as the park does. However, without a community to act as a permanent control, the two-thirds of the Island which is park would become a disaster area during the summer months of overcrowding and the other third a defensive enclave. That wouldn't be a healthy situation: the land would be used—perhaps even enjoyed —but it wouldn't be *lived in*. No matter how protected artificially by bureaucracy and money, basically it would be up for grabs, and I'm just bitter enough to think that land which is up for grabs nowadays is doomed.

As I've said, the key to the presence of a permanent community is the school. For the Island's year-round population to include the necessary young couples there must be a school, and, conversely, if there are no children in any one year the school closes and is difficult to reopen. From here on the problem is economic. For the fisherman, the old advantage of proximity to the fishing grounds has been canceled out by the high-powered marine engine, and what remains is the disadvantage of being farther from the market than the competition. The scallop fishing is improving; but lobstering is still the basic fishery, and the general scarcity of lobsters seems to be growing—perhaps not even as one part of a cycle but in a steady decline toward at least a temporary extinction of the species. This hits everybody on the coast, but the margin of acceptability on the Island is slimmer; after a while, a man and his family would have to leave, and there would be less likelihood of another family replacing them. There is no possibility of farming, as the soil is practically one solid ledge. Even if the islanders wanted to encourage tourism, which they don't, there isn't enough money to be made in the two possible months to last a family the rest of the

year without turning the place into a down east Disneyland. The worst thing is
that the wage earner can't range out for other work (or any work at all) when
times are bad and return home at night, as he can on the mainland. The Island
is geographically limited, and so the economic possibilities are limited. On top
of this, it costs more to live on the Island as the cost of transportation is either
tacked on to the price of things or paid directly.

As more and more people have bought or built vacation houses on the coast,
the price of shorefront land has gone wild, even where there is any available.
This phenomenon was foreseeable, and most of the non-park land on the Island
was bought up by a few of the summer people. This was for reasons of conservation, but the effect has been to drive up the price of land on the Island way
beyond the means of a young family who would want to settle. At least one of
the summer residents has recognized the self-defeat in this and has let it be
known that he has land to sell, but *only* to a family with schoolchildren, come
with the intention of settling down.

Someone who knows and loves the Island well spoke of the "critical mass"
necessary to make the community function, by which he meant the necessary
minimum number of families fishing all or most of the year. He put the number
at three, as he felt the pressure of singularity would be too much for even just
two; at this writing, there are nine fishing boats, of which two are going scalloping in the winter. The problem is that when the population gets so close to
the bare minimum you can never be sure that there isn't just one person who is
really keeping the community going, whose identity will not be known until he
is gone and the place falls apart.

The best description of the quality of Maine I have ever read is an article by
Elizabeth Hardwick, "In Maine," published in the October 7, 1971, issue of
The New York Review of Books. It is immensely sad in its conclusion. I don't
feel the conclusions, although everything that she says on the way to them
seems profoundly true to me.

There is about the region a curious and fascinating softness that seems to spread
like a blanket over the hardness of rock and woods and icy turf. This is a
perturbation, this ambiguous softness in the drifting fogs, the thick greens of
the trees, the dampness, the swampy meadows. It is in the people too, in the men
as well as the women. Not a tropical softness, of course, but the odd snowy
lassitude of isolation. Whole countries and people formed by these long, huddling
winters. "Well," he told me, "November is the suicide season. Summer is over,
winter's ahead. Long months of closing in." Pregnancies, breakdowns.

"Oh, when I think of winter I just think of poverty spread over everything. The cold makes everything poor. They are always saying they like it, like it the best of all, calling it better than summer. But I don't think they are telling the truth. . . . I think winter does something to your head, your feeling, something not even the summer's heat can undo." And he looked with a soft melancholy toward the waving sea. "Well, anyway, this is a handsome place."

I've described my winter on the Island as active and even joyous, but perhaps that had a lot to do with purpose and novelty—certainly I wasn't on all winter long. I know I felt the soft despair as a *possibility* around me all the time, and I felt it directly nearly every time I went down into Rich's Cove. On the other hand, the islanders are bound by geography into a heroic unit of resistance to the slough of despond. They are never really alone because enough people must always be wondering in bad times how the folks down on the Island are getting along, as they sit out there conspicuously. But the winters are still long and bleak and pervasive.

I have the feeling that the energy leading to community action which might ease the economic difficulties and thereby stabilize or even increase the population is controlled by a kind of social thermostat. The Island—or anyway a majority of the population—prefers to remain calm in the face of its difficulties, community action comes hard, and community noise is frowned on. When the problem reaches a certain point of crisis, the thermostat triggers group action, which probably is true of any community. However, on the Island, there is a thermostat control in the opposite direction, set not very much higher than the crisis setting, which cuts off action immediately after the crisis has passed, but perhaps before the problem has been thrashed out to a solution. Only that which saves the community from utter ruin is done and no more so that the Island doesn't get overheated. Although this is done out of the (unstated) conviction that the community's greatest strength is its ability to live together, there are a few who believe that the cutoff control is set too low.

There is no way of judging the effect of the summer community on the Island because it has existed for such a long time, but it must be true that the annual summer infusion of outside ideas and talent, not to mention money, has and will continue to help. A Canadian friend points out that New Brunswick, an area which is even poorer than Maine, has always been separated from the other provinces, even in the summer, and seems hopeless in its poverty, whereas Maine seems to him far from hopeless. He lays the difference to the annual challenge of the summer visitors—or at least to the fact of less isolation. Out of

Phil, hauling a trap onto the washboard

Measuring a lobster

The weir at high tide. The twine of one lead extends to the shore.

The weir at low tide, with herring in the pound and the pumper alongside
The hose of the pumper sucking up the herring

Jack MacDonald's lobster boat, rigged for scalloping, on a winter evening

Emptying the drags
Cleaning a scallop

Jack MacDonald, watching the fathometer and feeling the boat during a drag

Summer

Boom Beach

It seems to me that the experience of the Island by summer residents of all ages is most like the experience of childhood in general—childhood being the time when we are aware of the fact that we are small in relation to the natural world.

The land and the sea are dominant. The water of the ocean is too cold to swim in or sail on casually, and so there are no long, essentially social, days at the beach and in or on the water. Instead there are major and minor adventures, explorations and projects within the big, beautiful environment—within the special light of the Maine coast penetrating the special houses. Most summers, this is usually the dense luminosity of fog or the intense clarity of the bright days—extreme in both cases.

The Island is a good place in which to grow up—to measure your growth over the long years of childhood against familiar trees, grass, mountains, houses, boats. Friends from the winter life come to visit you in this special place (in their eyes, special to *you*), and you're proud. Alone, the place encloses you.

Growing up in the summers here, you would have to be different than if you had spent summers elsewhere, even if you never returned.

Inside the Wilsons' house

Miss Lizzie's birthday party
Summer family joke

Inside a house on the Point

A Point cottage

Stairwell of a Point cottage

The church

Base of a spruce

The York Island sheep drive

Sheep moving along the outer shore of York Island

Wayne Barter

Bob and Gerri Turner
Ted Hoskins and Mark Connors

Aside from the occasional picnics, there is an Island clambake toward the end of each August. The first summer I was on, the proceeds went to the purchase of playground equipment for the school.

The weekly dance